LEADING FROM THE JUMPSEAT

LEADING FROM THE JUMPSEAT

HOW TO CREATE EXTRAORDINARY OPPORTUNITIES
— BY HANDING OVER CONTROL —

PETER DOCKER

WHY NOT PRESS

Why Not Press
The Brewhouse
Priory Lane
Burford
Oxfordshire
OX18 4SG
United Kingdom

For discounted bulk purchase or personalized corporate editions, please email press@leadingfromthejumpseat.com

ISBN: 978-1-7399240-3-4 US paperback
ISBN: 978-1-7399240-6-5 US hardcover
ISBN: 978-1-7399240-4-1 international edition
ISBN: 978-1-7399240-5-8 international edition (2)
ISBN: 978-1-7399240-1-0 audiobook
ISBN: 978-1-7399240-2-7 e-book

Printed in the United States of America
10 9 8 7 6 5 4 3 2 1

Some names and characteristics have been changed to protect the privacy of the individuals involved.

Typeset by Catherine Williams, Chapter One Book Production

Cover design by Kaveh Haerian

Edited by Ilsa Hawtin and Georgina Fradgley

To all those who choose to lift others up

Contents

Belonging

❖

Chapter 1

Setting the Context

As a PILOT, I know that in the air things can change rapidly. One moment everything is calm and relaxed, then in the next you can be using every ounce of your skill and experience to stay alive. Fortunately, on large passenger jets this abrupt switch doesn't happen very often at all. One bright morning in August 2002 was one of those times when it did.

We had just taken off from San Francisco International Airport – with 140 men, women, and children on board – when we hit severe turbulence. In an instant, the aircraft went from smooth flight to being thrown around in the air like a rag doll, the turbulence caused perhaps by the wind passing over the nearby hills or by the wake of a jumbo jet ahead of us.

If we had been at the normal cruising height for a jumbo, 35,000 feet, this level of turbulence would have been very unpleasant indeed. Drinks would have been spilled. Some overhead lockers may have burst open. Any passengers without lap straps secured would have been lifted from their seats, some would have suffered bruises, and most would have been at best badly shaken before the plane found its way back into smooth air.

However, when this turbulence hit us, we were not at cruising height. Having just taken off, at a height of only 500 feet, the stakes were much higher. The possibility of us hitting the ground was very real.

As captain of the aircraft, the actions I took on the flight deck in the next few fleeting moments would directly affect whether everyone on that plane survived. Only, I wasn't in the captain's seat, nor was I in the copilot's seat. I didn't even have my hands on the controls. I was sitting in the jumpseat.

For anyone who's not familiar: the jumpseat is the extra seat on the flight deck, normally used only for observation purposes. There's strict etiquette on who can use the jumpseat – for example, an additional pilot, cabin attendant, or other crew member – depending on circumstances and requirements. That day I was therefore in the seat immediately behind the guy who *did* have his hands on the controls: Calum. I had signed him off as a fully qualified captain just the night before.

The previous day had been the culmination of several months' training for Calum. A talented young pilot in his late twenties, he had gone through the conversion from copilot to captain without a hitch. We were both officers in the Royal Air Force, and I was his squadron commander – his senior boss.

Over the couple of days before this flight, I had completed Calum's final assessment, acting as his copilot as we flew our military VC10 passenger jet from the UK to Washington Dulles and then on to San Francisco. During those flights, I had carefully monitored all aspects of his performance, and it had been clear to me he was comfortably up to standard. After we had completed the final shutdown at San Francisco, I had given Calum the great news: he was now fully qualified and was clear to fly, unsupervised, as a captain. This meant that on his next flight, leaving San Francisco, he would be fully accountable for the operation and safety of the entire aircraft, passengers, and crew, as aircraft captain on the flight back to Dulles. He would have a regular copilot joining him, supporting him on the flight deck. My job of training and certifying Calum was done. I would be down the back with the passengers, catching up on some paperwork.

The morning rush hour at San Francisco International is always hectic. There are four intersecting runways, which all meet in the middle, with dozens of aircraft jockeying for a take-off slot between arriving jets, accompanied by the near-constant, clipped chatter on the radios between pilots and air controllers. As an aircraft captain you need to be on top of your game.

An hour or so before our departure, I was enjoying leafing through an old copy of *Flight International*, while Calum and his crew were busy checking the weather, passenger load, routing, and fuel requirements for our trip to Dulles. Just before we were due to walk out to the aircraft, Calum came over to ask if I would be willing to sit in the jumpseat for taxi and take-off. We didn't fly from San Francisco very often, and he wanted an extra pair of eyes as we navigated our way around the busy taxiways to the runway. I willingly accepted his invitation and remember admiring his decision – it's a sound principle to take advantage of any "spare" crew members who can assist.

With pre-flight checks complete and passengers boarded, we taxied from the ramp. From the jumpseat I had an excellent view over the nose of the aircraft and was able to help identify the unfamiliar and potentially confusing network of taxiways as we took our place in line ready for take-off. It would have been easy for Calum to have taken a wrong turn, get out of sequence, and end up with a long delay as air traffic control pushed us to the back of the queue. But he was absolutely on top of it all, as I'd known he would be. Soon we were lined up on the runway, on time, cleared for departure.

As the engines howled and we thundered along the tarmac, there was no warning of what was about to happen. Everything seemed normal.

When the turbulence hit, on the flight deck we experienced the same sudden mayhem as the passengers. Pens, paper, and anything else loose was immediately tossed around. I could feel my own body straining against the straps that held me tightly in my seat. Meanwhile, Calum was doing his utmost to keep the aircraft flying away from the ground, working hard to keep the nose up and the wings level.

Seated in the jumpseat, watching Calum wrestle with the controls, I had a number of options. What's more, I knew my response in that moment could have a significant impact on the outcome of the whole situation, and I had barely a second to decide what to do. My response needed to be near-instinctive.

While I realize the chances are you're not a professional aviator, I'm going to ask you to take a moment to imagine what you might have done in my position. As the most experienced and senior pilot on the aircraft, you might have realized you needed to reach over and take control – after all, the lives of 140 people depended on what happened next. One notch down from that, maybe you would have thought it better to hold back but to give Calum advice on what to do. Perhaps you would have opted to call out words of encouragement over the crew intercom, helping to bolster Calum's confidence, and reassuring him on the actions he took. Or maybe you have another clear picture in your mind of how you would have reacted.

Take the wrong action and it could seriously affect everyone's chances of survival.

So, what will it be? Don't forget, you have only a couple of seconds to decide, and the clock is ticking ...

While you think about this scenario, I'm going to tell you about another story that has helped inspire me to write this book.

Fast forward sixteen years. It's 21st November 2018, and I've stopped at the side of the road for the third time, sitting staring at the steering wheel.

In 2007, after almost a quarter of a century, I'd left the Royal Air Force and chosen a path very different from my flying and military career. For the first few years, I'd worked for a consultancy in London. In the six years leading up to 2018, I had become a professional speaker and facilitator, delivering talks on leadership and business culture. I'd been supporting senior leadership teams around the world in pretty much every industry you can imagine. I was used to presenting regularly before crowds of thousands, with just a flipchart to help share ideas. And yet here I was, stopped at the side of the road on my way to give a talk to fewer than a hundred people, seriously considering turning around and going home. To say I felt nervous is an understatement.

Thinking about it rationally, this gig should have been a piece of cake. It was to all the RAF squadron commanders – the people who lead the main flying units of the air force. I had been a squadron commander myself, and I would likely know many of those in the audience and the challenges they faced.

The problem was the voice inside my head.

After retiring from the service, I had largely lost touch with anyone who still wore the uniform. Over the years, I had also picked apart how I'd led during my time in the military, thinking about how I might have done things better, if only I had known everything that I had learned in subsequent leadership roles. Now I was going to be talking to people I admired more than any others – people whose culture of camaraderie, courage, and selflessness I had once shared during all my time in the armed forces. I felt imposter syndrome creeping in – the idea I'd succeeded only due to luck and not because of any talent. I was very unsure of the reception I would get. The voice inside my head was telling me I really didn't want to find out.

It was the voice of fear.

There was another voice too – a voice that was telling me I had no option but to continue. I knew deep down that my ideas were worth sharing and might actually help those listening to think differently. And besides, I'd made a promise to do this, so there was just no way I could back out.

Fortunately, that second voice was louder. I checked my mirror for traffic, pulled out, and drove on.

When I arrived at the venue, everyone had just broken for coffee and gathered at the far end of the room. I entered quietly, said hello to the organizers, and busied myself setting up. I'd been there about five minutes when I felt a hand on my shoulder and was relieved when I turned around to see the beaming face of an old friend and colleague. Simon had been a junior officer on my squadron back in 2004, and here he was now, promoted and commanding his own squadron. He shook my hand warmly, wanting to know what I'd been up to since we'd last met. Simon was closely followed by several others, all keen to shake my hand and welcome me. Instantly, I felt embraced. More than that, I felt I belonged.

The presentation went well. Any nerves I had quickly evaporated as I felt the support from the whole room. Everyone seemed engaged and keen to hear what I had to say, and they asked some excellent questions too. This reminded me that learning is a large part of the military culture – something that is often less present in the civilian world. When it was time to wrap up, I took a moment to explain to everyone how I'd felt on my drive up that morning. I thanked the organizer for giving me the opportunity to overcome those fears, and everyone there for welcoming me back into the fold.

After my presentation, we gathered in the bar for a formal dinner and the opportunity to chat. Simon came over to continue our earlier conversation, and we were soon joined by two others, Phil and Al. Like Simon, they had been junior officers on my squadron and now had their own squadrons to lead. I warmly congratulated all three men on the progress they had made and the positions they now held.

What came next took me completely by surprise. Without any hesitation, and in unison, they replied, "We owe it all to you."

I was left speechless and feeling more humbled than ever before or since in my life. I could never have expected those words from men I had worked with so many years earlier, let alone after I'd felt such an imposter while driving to this event.

Those six words from Simon, Phil, and Al have led to a lot of consideration of what I might have done wrong – as well as what I must have got right – during my time in the armed forces. They've helped shape my thinking around inspiring leaders across the world since that day.

Let's go back now to that flight from San Francisco. I'll tell you how I decided to act in those split seconds shortly after a potentially disastrous take-off ...

I did absolutely nothing.

I remained in my seat, perfectly relaxed, with my hands resting in my lap, keeping completely silent.

I knew that Calum could handle the situation. If I'd had any doubts, I would have had no business signing him off as a captain the previous day. For me to have intervened in any way would have risked confusing the crew and dangerously affecting the outcome.

In that moment, I needed to become a great *follower.* In that moment, I started to appreciate the importance of Leading from the Jumpseat.

—— Chapter 2 ——

Why Jumpseat Leadership?

EVERYTHING IN THIS book is a distillation of what I have been lucky enough to learn about leadership throughout my time as a professional pilot, military commander, project manager, negotiator, teacher, speaker, consultant, and father. Please note that there is no reason that father comes last on that list. As you will learn from various examples in this book, I consider the role of parent to be sometimes the most challenging and rewarding, and often the greatest test of one's ability to Lead from the Jumpseat.

I've had the opportunity to lead – and follow – in many challenging situations. At times I have felt completely out of my depth. At other times I've achieved outcomes way beyond what I would have predicted or even hoped for. I've worked with many extraordinary practitioners and leaders around the world, and some frankly dreadful ones too. Each has left their mark on me and I wouldn't change any of it.

This book is the opportunity to reflect, bring everything together, and share what I have learned. I firmly believe that every person and every organization is capable of accomplishing extraordinary things, achieving way more than they may even think is possible. The key is first to connect with who we truly are, at a human level.

Sometimes we can see the effect we have on the world and on others almost immediately. As pilots, the choices we make often fall into this category and can be a great test of leadership, as illustrated by the first story in Chapter 1. The second story in that chapter is an illustration of how it can sometimes take years for us to realize the effect we have on those around us.

For me, the flight deck of a large aircraft is like a microcosm of leadership. It's an environment that can uncover the very best and very worst examples of how human beings interact and perform, particularly while under pressure. The team that makes up a flight crew is always changing. As part of a large airline, the first time that crew members meet one another will often be scarcely an hour before departure. Despite this, they always need to be able to work effectively together, particularly if faced with an emergency within the first few minutes of flight.

Perhaps the most dramatic example of this over recent years was a US Airways flight on 15th January 2009. Flown by Captain Chesley Sullenberger and his first officer, Jeffrey Skiles, this crew was forced to ditch the aircraft in the Hudson River barely six minutes after taking off from LaGuardia Airport. Remarkably, everyone survived, thanks to the skill of the pilots and the professionalism of the cabin crew, and with all of them working together. The incident became known as the "Miracle on the Hudson".

While the story I told at the beginning of the book is less dramatic and the outcome less miraculous, it's still clear Calum did indeed save the day. After recovering from the turbulence, we all continued our flight safely to Washington Dulles. Calum's training played an essential part in the outcome, as did his character as an individual, combined with the culture of our organization.

I am confident that how I chose to respond helped too. Most of us have experienced how it feels to know that someone else believes in us and has our back. It helps us overcome nagging hesitation or self-doubt, especially when we encounter something new or particularly challenging. The belief others have in us accelerates us forward in a way that can rarely be achieved on our own.

Later in our flight to Dulles, after handing control to the other pilot, Calum took a break to stretch his legs and joined me in the galley over a cup of tea. I congratulated him on how he'd calmly and effectively handled the situation earlier. He looked down the aisle at all the passengers and quietly reflected, "I now know what it means to be a captain."

Leading from the Jumpseat is a metaphor for how we can choose to lead and the culture we can create. It's about the journey we take to get to the point where we hand over control to other people, who are then able to continue to move forward without us. It's about lifting people up and giving them the space they need so that, when the time is right, they can take the lead. This is a higher form of leadership, since it is not about building and retaining our own individual power. Instead, it focuses on nurturing the potential of others and empowering them to become leaders. All of this is especially important if we're working on something that really matters to us. I'll explain why in Chapter 3.

In business and in life, handing over the reins to others is inevitable. Everyone will eventually leave their team, retire from being the CEO, or see their kids leave home and lead their own lives. Leading from the Jumpseat enables us to embrace this inevitability. It encourages leadership to develop at every level within our teams. It empowers our people to perform better together and leads to us accomplishing more. It creates a culture that is generative and supportive. It's an approach that nurtures the underlying conditions so that what we have built will continue to grow.

Leading from the Jumpseat is a practice. It's a way of interacting with others that will enhance performance in any given situation – during normal business, times of crisis, and life in general. It equips us to confront daunting challenges. It gives us the mindset to reach beyond what we currently know how to do, with the commitment to figure out the answers as we go.

Reflection is important. It was not until years after that flight with Calum that I realized what Jumpseat Leadership truly is and that I had been learning it all along. You see, if we succeed as Jumpseat Leaders, while the effect on others is immediate, there's a good chance we may not know about it ourselves until years later. When I hesitated on the drive up to give my talk to the squadron commanders, it was because I didn't know how I would be received after my years away. I was unsure what legacy I had left behind, if any at all. Looking back, it seems to me I had in fact managed to become a

Jumpseat Leader – after all, Simon, Phil, and Al (to name a few) have continued to rise as leaders in their own right. I've no doubt they will accomplish more than I have. And that, surely, is a legacy worth having.

—— CONSIDER THIS ——

With each chapter of this book, I want to offer some simple ways to get into action using the ideas I've shared. How we get into action will depend on where we are personally on our Jumpseat Leadership journey. In each chapter I'll break that journey down into four stages.

The first stage is when we're trying to identify what's really most important to us – what matters and what doesn't. At this stage we're learning how to lead ourselves. I'll call this **Learning to fly**.

Alternatively, we might already be firmly on our journeys in life, putting into action those things that are really important to us, and building resilience that will help us continue to do so. We are now beginning to think more about others and how our actions affect the bigger picture. I'll call this stage **Flying**.

Next there is **Teaching others to fly**. This is when we are holding the space for others to grow, so they can consolidate what's important to them and make a greater contribution to the team and, ultimately, to the world. We're passing on our knowledge and expertise, while also making that transition to leading those who have skills and expertise that extend beyond our own.

Finally, there is **Leading from the Jumpseat**. This is when we are focused on creating the conditions where others can take the controls, just as I was able to do for Calum, Simon, Phil, and Al. We are ready and willing to adopt the role of "follower", to follow and support those we have lifted up. We know when we're getting it right if we're welcomed back – if we're invited in by those we have helped to take the lead.

Each of the four stages reflects how we might lead at different times in our working careers as we, for example, progress and reach increasingly senior positions in a company. However, the stage we're at is not necessarily linked to only one position or role. For example, as an entrepreneur, while your role as founder might not change, you will likely experience each of the four stages as you grow your business, until you ultimately sell it, retire, or simply stop breathing. It's the same as being a parent: we will experience all of the stages in turn, from the first days when we're trying to figure out how to take care of a newborn, all the way through to when our children have grown up, left home, and are leading their own lives.

It's also worth remembering that we will sometimes experience different stages at any one time in our lives. For example, there will be times when we're only just starting a new work role but are leading in a role outside of work.

Whatever we are doing, we never stop learning. For all these reasons, I encourage you to look at all the chapters and examples in this book.

—— COMMITMENT ——

—— Chapter 3 ——

When Something is Important Enough

WHAT DO YOU really care about? I'm not talking about your new car, your latest mobile phone, or your next pay rise. While those sorts of things are important at some level – and we can all get upset if they are damaged, lost, or never seen – we can probably survive without them. What I'm referring to are **those things that really matter to us**. The things that, like a constant background hum, guide our actions throughout life. Those things that are non-negotiable. Those for which we will willingly hold our ground – defend against the odds – even when that requires personal sacrifice.

For many of us, one aspect of our lives that we care deeply about is family. Another is our closest friends. Chances are, if we feel that those close to us are threatened or sick, or in some other way need our help, we will do everything possible to step up to the mark and support them. For example, last year I received a call from my wife saying she'd been involved in a car accident. I dropped everything I was doing and immediately went to help. Nothing would have stopped me. Of course, this had consequences: work didn't get done and conference calls were missed. But later, when I explained the reasons to those I'd let down, there was complete understanding. Everybody got it, without my needing to apologize further. Such is the near-universal acceptance that family really matters.

What's interesting is the power and momentum released inside of us when we're faced with something we care deeply about. We become energized to overcome any obstacle in our way, even when we're not sure of what to do. This is perhaps particularly so for parents, whether they're protecting their children from physical harm or giving them every possible opportunity to thrive. We only have to see the often distressing images of parents clutching their young children tightly as they flee war zones to recognize how powerful this drive can be.

While the importance of family and close friends is perhaps a given, it can take us a while to begin to understand what else calls to us as individuals and just how important those things are. It can take even longer to fully, consciously process and accept these thoughts, to turn an understanding of what matters most into a concrete foundation for life. Some people start to realize this process in their early teens. For others it might not be until their later years, prompted perhaps by a life-changing event, that what's most important becomes completely clear. The point is, the sooner we can identify what really, *truly* matters most to us, the sooner we can tap into the energy and drive those things provide.

This reserve of energy is important for anyone who chooses to lead. Whenever we are leading, we are able to create and steer things in ways that wouldn't otherwise have happened. Leadership is therefore often about bringing new things into existence – things that wouldn't have occurred if we weren't in that role.

By its very nature, leadership is difficult. We live in a complex world in which our actions often have unpredictable outcomes. This is particularly so when we interact with other human beings. Unlike lines of computer code, where one instruction logically follows another, human behaviour delivers infinitely different, unexpected consequences.

As leaders, we will face new and challenging situations in which we will often have no reliable or consistent way of knowing where to start or which route to take. To make headway as a leader, it's therefore vital first to find an anchor in those things that are most important to us. An anchor in our foundation, built of the things we hold as truly important in life. Whenever we are met with the most difficult leadership situations, those things will then act as the source of energy we can draw from to overcome the challenges we face. Once we know deep down what is really important to us, it will also help guide the choices we make and how we lead ourselves. And the better we lead ourselves, the better equipped we become to lead others.

CHOICES ARE THE CLUES

For most people, one of the earliest significant choices we have to make in life is what to do after leaving school. For some, this can be quite straightforward. We may have had a long-held desire – some may see it as a "calling" – to be, say, a doctor, a lawyer, or an engineer. None of these careers is easy to qualify for, let alone succeed in. While it's easy to assume that people who follow a path into the performing arts would have things easier, they will likely confront more disappointment and rejection than most, no matter how skilled they become. Whatever the field, those who do succeed will be driven by something deep inside – something that has required personal sacrifices over many years of training. That drive will have enabled them to overcome the setbacks along the way.

While we're making our first career choices, there will likely be close friends and family members who say things like, "Are you *sure* about this?", "It's going to be tough and will cost a lot", or "You should look at going into marketing instead – you'd be great at that". Those people who choose not to embrace further education or other formal training may face pressure from family members who think they're making the wrong decision, or – sometimes worse – the unspoken rejection from high school friends who have conformed to others' expectations. Some people might believe they have brilliant new business ideas but be scorned by others who think they'll never be successful. Whatever the circumstances, when we make key choices, there will no doubt be those around us who have different opinions. But there will be plenty of us who plough ahead anyway with our choices because they feel like the right thing to do.

Back in September 1981, I'd made my choice to start at Keele University on a double degree in electronic engineering and computing. There were certainly a lot of folks who were sceptical about the path I selected. I'd had very little tuition in electronics, and computing was yet to become mainstream (which gives you an idea of my vintage). In my last two years of high school, I'd focused on mathematics (which would help a little), English literature, and economics. Such was my lack of relevant academic background that Keele was the only university at the time willing to offer me a place. My reasoning for choosing this path? I'd convinced myself that the future lay in my chosen field of study, and this would be where many well-paid opportunities would open up. Looking back, I was interested in, but not particularly passionate about, these subjects. For me, this was more about being determined to pay my way in the world and not being a burden on anyone else. Even at that age, self-reliance was starting to emerge as something that was very important to me.

I was seven months into my degree when Argentinian forces invaded the Falkland Islands in the South Atlantic Ocean, some 8,000 miles away from my relatively serene university campus. It was a bid by Argentina to reclaim sovereignty of the small and rugged archipelago, home to several thousand people, which had been a British overseas territory for well over a century. The Falkland Islanders considered themselves very much British (as they still do) and did not welcome the new regime, which had been abruptly imposed upon them. At the time of the invasion, I didn't know the history of the longstanding dispute between Britain and Argentina, but there was one aspect that really resonated with me: I felt incensed that people were being forced down a path against their will. The islanders were helpless against the overwhelming force of troops that had arrived on their land, sent by a government that did not respect the way they had chosen to live.

I realized I wanted to be in a position to do something about it – if not for those in the Falklands, then for others in similar situations in the future. The Falklands invasion crystallized in my mind something that was central to me: I wanted to help those who were unable to help themselves.

Growing up, through youth organizations and family connections, I'd had a long association with the Royal Air Force. Now I figured that, by joining this organization, I would become part of something that matched my own ethos. By June 1983 I'd made another choice that many questioned at the time: I'd left university, in the middle of my degree, and started my training as an RAF officer and pilot at the military college, Cranwell.

My choices were beginning to turn into *stands*.

POSITIONS AND STANDS

When we have an agreed understanding of what a word means – a distinction – it enables us to have different conversations, which can enable us to achieve better results. For example, back in 2019 relatively few people knew what a Zoom call was. Today, millions of us share that distinction.

One distinction I have found particularly helpful is the difference between a position and a stand.

A **position** is *against* something – a negative reaction to something we don't agree with. We hear about this a lot these days in politics, in the news, and especially on social media. That's largely because it's relatively easy to say what we don't agree with, to object to an idea or another person's view. We can find ourselves triggered when we hear or read a comment we particularly don't like. We experience a feeling that comes from somewhere deep inside, which seems to rise up from the stomach. But the very existence of a position depends on its *counter-position*. In other words, take that counter-position away and our position can no longer survive.

Let me give you an example.

Imagine you're driving along a narrow street and you meet a car coming the other way. There's not enough room for both cars, so either you or the other driver will need to back up and let the other pass. However, each of you takes up the position that the other driver needs to give way. Tempers rise, and you become more entrenched in your conviction that the other guy needs to move. You rationalize to yourself to reinforce your position: *He was driving too fast; his car is way wider than it needs to be; my journey is more important than his.* However, as these and other thoughts race through your head, you suddenly notice that the other driver is reversing back to a passing place to allow you to continue. The position you had so quickly taken and started to reinforce in your mind immediately dissolves.

A **stand**, on the other hand, is *for* something and generates an entirely different energy. A stand does not depend on anyone or anything else to exist. It's about what *you* believe is important. A stand is like an island on which you have planted your flag to show what you stand for. Those sailing past your island can see your flag and, if they share the same belief, they can come and join you on your island – there's room for everyone. Importantly, if anyone doesn't share your stand, they can sail on by, and that really is okay. Whatever others choose to do, your stand can remain in existence for as long as you decide to hold it.

How would this play out in our narrow street example? Let's say the driver who backed up had a stand for courtesy and consideration on the roads. This stand does not depend on the actions of the driver in the other car, and it will still exist long after that particular moment has passed. It will also feel pretty good to practise that stand. The energy it releases is positive.

The objective of a position is to triumph over the counter-position. It is inherently divisive, can become exhausting, and is dependent on others maintaining their counter-position.

The objective of a stand is to become more consistent and stronger in a belief you hold. It requires you to be willing, if necessary, to make sacrifices to support your belief, while always being open to others who choose to join you in that stand. It is generative, inclusive, and does not rely on others to exist.

Although I didn't fully realize it at the time, when I chose to leave university and join the RAF, I was taking a stand to help people who were otherwise defenceless. It was something I felt was the right thing to do. Having this stand drove me forward, regardless of others who may have doubted my choice. Taking a stand – acting on what we believe is right – often demands courage, as we are very likely to "stand out". It's also often an act of vulnerability, as we are letting others in on what really matters to us.

A great friend of mine, known simply as AJ, served with me in the RAF, and we have now been close for several decades. Throughout that time, he's always chosen not to drink alcohol. It must have been tough for him as a young guy, as we both were back in the 1980s, when there was quite a strong drinking culture among our peers. But AJ had the courage to stick consistently to what he believed to be the best choice, and people respected him for it. Importantly, he never made out that other people were wrong for not sharing his stand – it was about him, not others. And this is one of the most important points about a stand: while at times it can take great courage to maintain a stand, the more consistent we are, the easier it becomes.

Taking a stand – deciding to be true to a strong belief – gives us a foundation for wiser and stronger decisions. It works as a guide, helping us to make better and more consistent decisions that feel right, and gives us the reserve of energy to see those decisions through. It thereby generates better and more consistent options in our lives, even when we are faced with another stand that seems to be inconsistent with our own.

CONFLICTING STANDS

When we have a stand, it is by definition something we care deeply about. It generates a lot of positive energy and we can become passionate about it. But what if we find ourselves in a situation with someone else who has a stand that seems to be in conflict with our own?

This is when we can easily drift into taking a position against the other person. When we do, the positive energy turns negative, which tends to close down possibility as we become focused on prevailing over the other person's beliefs. A better way to make progress again is to get back to our own stand.

When my son was approaching his eighteenth birthday, he decided he wanted to graduate from riding his small-engined moped and buy a large 600cc Suzuki Bandit motorcycle. This machine was capable of accelerating from 0 to 60 mph in a little over three seconds and could hit a top speed of 130 mph. As a parent, my immediate reaction was to think, *No way is that happening!* The roads near to where we live are dangerous. They're narrow, twisty, and frequently congested with vehicles that all survive better in an accident than a motorcycle. Like just about any parent, the safety and well-being of my children is really important to me.

However, my son had a different view. What was really important to him was freedom – the freedom to get around to see his friends and enjoy the excitement of speed. The predictable outcome of our differing views would have been my son and me ending up locked in position versus counter-position. We would then have become like the example of the two cars on the narrow street, only this time with neither party willing to give way.

I chose a different approach.

Rather than taking up a position *against* my son having the Suzuki, I refocused on my stand *for* him being safe. This simple shift gave me an entirely new perspective and led to an alternative conversation. I told him I would support his choice and even help him find a good second-hand motorcycle. However, there was one condition: he needed to agree to extend his training beyond the minimum required to gain his licence. On qualifying, he would immediately enrol in a school to become a certified advanced motorcyclist. I told him I would pay for the additional training, and what's more, I would follow the same programme and learn alongside him. My son agreed. After all, he reckoned it would be cool to become an advanced rider.

We started the training, and we even bought a beautiful yellow Bandit, which sat in our shed waiting until we were qualified to ride it. And then, a few weeks into the training, my son came to me and said he'd decided on a different path. He said he had worked out that he wouldn't be able to afford to go anywhere on the Suzuki because, at his age, the cost of insurance would be extortionate. He'd decided to buy a car instead.

Over the weeks this unfolded, our relationship took on a new dimension as we trained together as equals. This would never have happened if I'd taken a position. Like many strong-minded teenagers, my son would have dug his heels in if I had insisted he wasn't allowed to ride a 600cc motorcycle. Thankfully, the fact that I took a stand instead allowed him to think openly about the pros and cons, including the cost of insurance. Soon after, he bought his car and very soon chose to gain his advanced car driver certification too. As for the Suzuki, we sold it in pristine condition a few months later, without it being ridden by either of us.

STANDS INTO ACTION

The stands we choose to take in life will guide our actions, building what others will see as important aspects of our character. What's more, people generally have heightened respect for anyone who has strong beliefs for positive reasons. The more consistency we have with our stands, the greater the trust others will feel towards us. When we extend those stands to guide us in our work or our business, they will also provide the foundation on which reputation is built.

Elon Musk, the South African–born American entrepreneur, has built several businesses based on those things that are most important to him. Perhaps the best known are his electric car company, Tesla, and his space exploration business, SpaceX. Both these companies are built on something Musk feels very strongly about: the future of the human race. This is one of his stands. Equally, he has a stand for making that future exciting, and he believes it won't happen unless we *make* it happen.

Tesla is based on a stand for making the mass uptake of electric vehicles an attractive and viable alternative to those that run on fossil fuels. Musk maintains this will reduce carbon emissions into the atmosphere and help ensure our planet remains habitable for the long term. Whether we share his belief or not doesn't matter to Musk. He is flying his flag on his island. He is open to others joining him if they wish. Alternatively, if they don't want to be a part of what he's building, they can sail on by.

In a little over a decade of Tesla mass-producing electric cars, many other vehicle manufacturers have committed to do the same. Musk has encouraged this, offering support, and the licensing of Tesla's technology, to other manufacturers. Rather than taking a position *against* the market competition, Musk continues to take a stand *for* the future he wants to create. He reiterated this on 29th July 2020, when he shared on Twitter, "We're just trying to accelerate sustainable energy, not crush competitors!"

SpaceX is another excellent example of Musk bringing a stand to life. When he formed the company in 2002, space exploration was the domain of government-funded programmes, not private companies. The role of SpaceX is to further Musk's stand for the future of the human race, by enabling us to eventually colonize Mars.

STANDS FUEL RESILIENCE

In 2006 SpaceX launched its first rocket. It exploded 33 seconds after lift-off. The second attempt, in 2007, also failed. As did the third, in 2008, which also destroyed the first payload to be carried for NASA. Fortunately, the fourth attempt went well and was followed by a run of other successful launches. Then, on 28th June 2015 – on Musk's birthday – a SpaceX rocket, carrying a double payload for NASA, vaporized shortly after launch.

Each of these failures must have been a body blow to Musk. And yet his stand has sustained him and kept him going. When once asked how he overcomes all the setbacks, Musk replied, "When something is important enough, you do it even if the odds are not in your favor."

As we build up understanding of ourselves and what really matters in our lives, it gives us the opportunity to tap into deep reserves of energy. This energy can propel us forward in the most challenging of times, helping us overcome the obstacles we meet. It can also sustain us when we fail along the way. Defining those things that are truly important to us as stands, rather than positions, enables us to consciously act on them in ways that are generative. To act on stands takes courage and, when we find that courage, we define who we are as individuals. Put simply, we start to *lead ourselves*. And when we do that, we have the reference points we need to more effectively lead others.

—— CONSIDER THIS ——

We are likely to develop several stands over our lifetime, reflecting those things that are really important to us. These stands will include how we treat our family, friends, and work colleagues; the choices we make about how we spend our time and money; and how we shape our plans for the future. Importantly, the clearer we become on our stands, the more useful they become in guiding us when we face the unknown.

◆ **LEARNING TO FLY**

Consider this: The next time you find yourself in a situation with someone else in which you can feel tension, stop and ask yourself, *Am I merely taking a counter-position, or is this something that really matters to me?*

If it's the latter, take steps to turn that position into a stand, so that you can work through whatever is in front of you towards a cooperative and positive outcome.

If it's the former and doesn't really matter to you, try dropping your position altogether and see what happens.

◆ FLYING

Consider this: Do those around you know what you stand for?

Consolidate your stands by practising them through the actions you take. Seek consistency. When facing a challenge, hold on to what's important to you to sustain you throughout the challenge. This will build character and resilience.

◆ TEACHING OTHERS TO FLY

Consider this: The next time you witness differing positions gearing up for a struggle, take the opportunity to intervene.

Ask questions. Listen for the underlying stands. Work with each side to uncover what they truly care about in the given situation to see if a simple solution presents itself.

If there are conflicting stands, brainstorm to find a generative solution so that each person can continue to take their stand.

◆ LEADING FROM THE JUMPSEAT

Consider this: The next time someone asks how you would deal with a given situation and you know they are equipped to deal with it themselves, kindly turn the question around on them.

Give the other person the opportunity to make decisions and lead, based on their own stands.

———— Chapter 4 ————

Cutting Through the Noise

LIVING IN OUR complex world considerably increases the challenges that confront us when we choose to lead. We can be faced with insufficient information, an overload of information, conflicting perspectives, constraints, uncertainty, doubt, and fear, to name only a few challenges. And that's before we even start to consider how any other people we're trying to lead will see a situation, and how those perceptions will shape *their* actions.

All these challenges show up wherever we go. This can be in the day-to-day running of a large global organization, when trying to be a great parent or, indeed, just leading ourselves. Wherever there are humans, there will be complexity.

Inevitably, there can be a lot of what I call **noise**, which can frustrate our progress. Noise is the stuff over which we have no control, or that detracts from what we should be focused on – those things that really matter. What we want to identify is the signal – the message, vision, mission, or cause – that everyone in our team can relate to and act upon. It's a bit like tuning in an old radio, trying to get rid of the crackle so we can clearly hear the radio station we want.

We all need to be on the same channel or, as we say, on the same wavelength.

Cutting through the noise to find the signal is about navigating our way through complexity to uncover the simplicity of what really matters. As Leonardo da Vinci said, "Simplicity is the greatest sophistication". Finding simplicity is not necessarily simple. But it is a task of a leader. Thankfully, when we draw on our stands – those things that are really important to us – they guide us to find the signal that becomes the clear message everyone can hear.

IN THE CENTRE OF THE DONUT

17th March 2003, in the sweltering heat of the Saudi Arabian desert, was one of the days on which it was absolutely critical I found the signal that everyone could hear.

I was the British force commander for the RAF's air-refuelling deployment to Prince Sultan Air Base, which is located in the desert about 100 miles south-east of Saudi Arabia's capital, Riyadh. This meant I would need to lead a team drawn from two flying squadrons, consisting of aircrew and aircraft, together with a large contingent of technicians from an engineering squadron. The technicians' job was to keep our 40-year-old VC10 aircraft serviceable. We were all part of the US-led, multinational coalition drawn together to unseat Saddam Hussein from power in Iraq. What followed would become known as the Iraq War, or the Second Gulf War.

The VC10 we flew was originally built in the 1960s as a large passenger jet. Capable of flying long distances, it had been converted to act as a "fuel station in the sky", able to deploy hoses from its wings to refuel fighter jets while airborne. From a military perspective, this was a vital capability – fighter jets typically have a very limited range, and being able to refuel without landing meant they could spend much more time in the air doing their job. Aircraft also have a maximum take-off weight, made up of fuel and payload. Being able to refuel once airborne meant the fighter jets could take off with less fuel and more weapons. They could then meet later in the sky with VC10s to get the gas they needed to complete their missions.

As for us in the VC10, we only carried fuel. We had no weapons or self-defence systems, and we relied on careful planning, the protection of fighter aircraft, and a degree of luck to avoid being shot down.

I had deployed with my team of around 180 people three weeks previously, and we had spent the time preparing for what increasingly seemed an inevitable war. My people were trained and knew what they would need to do. But I had a major challenge caused by events outside my control.

As we readied for war, thousands of people were demonstrating across the world against the imminent conflict. Large crowds gathered in London, New York, Paris, and many other cities, to express how wrong they felt military action would be. Many headlines in the British press mirrored that feeling, while the United Nations Security Council raised questions about the legality of what President Bush and Prime Minister Blair were proposing. Some of us in uniform likely had our doubts too, but as part of the military, you cannot pick and choose your involvement. You do your duty.

At the airbase we had access to the news via satellite television, so it was inevitable my team followed each development as it unfolded. The latest update was that the British cabinet minister, Robin Cook, had resigned from the government in protest against the military action the prime minister seemed ready to order.

For military people about to put themselves in harm's way, it's very unsettling to sense the public isn't behind you or that the government to whom you answer is divided. When I was a young officer involved in the 1991 Gulf War, the situation seemed much clearer: Iraq had invaded Kuwait, and we were part of the multinational coalition drawn together to liberate the country from Iraqi forces. Now, in 2003, it was much less clear-cut. There was a lot of noise that could undermine my people and distract them from their job. And that's when lives can be put at even greater risk. I had to find the signal – the simple message – that could cut through the complexity and provide focus for us all.

On the morning of 17th March we had scheduled a photo shoot to capture everyone on the detachment – my team of aircrew, engineers, and support staff. In the searing desert sunshine, we arranged ourselves in a relatively pleasing manner in front of one of our aircraft, with the photographer perched slightly precariously at the top of a ladder. After the photograph, I knew it was the time for me to say something. We would likely be in the throes of battle in a matter of days, and I was highly conscious some of my people might not survive. I needed to find some words of guidance or encouragement. But I hadn't been in this situation before.

With no great speech prepared, I nonetheless gathered every-one around in the shape of a donut, with me in the centre. In silence, I paused for a moment as I turned slowly around, looking each individual in the eyes. I then went with my gut and started speaking.

First, I turned to my aircraft maintenance engineers. I told them their job was to keep these old aircraft serviceable and ready for every mission so the aircrew could do their job. I turned next to the aircrew and support team, telling them their job was to fly every mission we were given, refuelling every fighter jet that needed us. In a matter-of-fact way, I reminded them, "If we don't refuel those jets, then our troops on the ground won't receive the air cover they need. And if they don't get air cover, our troops on the ground will die."

At this moment everyone became tuned in. The volume of the noise was turned down – literally and figuratively – allowing the signal to come through loud and clear. You could have heard a pin drop as the importance of what each of us needed to do sank in.

I had created simplicity by capturing, at a human level, why we needed to do our job – to protect those British, American, and Australian troops we had never met and yet who depended on us to play our part in protecting them. I later wrote about my impromptu speech in my personal journal, recalling, "I said a few words that were probably not that inspiring". However, my team seemed to become even more energized and focused. With those words I had managed to cut through all the noise of what was going on politically and in the media, while also quelling team gossip and unexpressed conversations.

Although I may not have recognized it at the time, I had spoken from my stand of supporting others who needed help, and perhaps had also helped others to tune in to this unifying cause. As it turned out, I'd likely landed on something that really mattered to everyone around me.

Now of course the wider complexity had still to be managed: complicated flying procedures, insufficient aircraft spare parts and equipment, the threat of being shot down, and being prepared for air raids on our base with biological or chemical attack. But this was all made easier because individuals had made a personal connection to what we had been called upon to do.

On numerous occasions, leadership emerged at every level. I saw technicians repairing aircraft outside in sandstorms, determined to have them ready for flight. I had at least one instance of a hardy and experienced engineer being almost in tears as they struggled to make a repair in time – they didn't want to be the one to let the team down. On another occasion, after completing their refuelling mission, a crew had to divert their flight to a secret military airbase that didn't exist on any charts, only to discover on landing that their aircraft had been damaged by enemy gunfire. Somehow they figured it out, managed to make temporary repairs, and launched the following morning on another refuelling mission.

Perhaps the most telling moment was when I had to decide which of my flight crews needed to be the first to swap with a new crew arriving from the UK. No one wanted to leave. No one wanted to be the first to leave our base in the desert before the operation was over.

Over the next four and a half months of the deployment, we were tasked with 479 missions. We flew 479 missions. Most important for me: when the operation was over, everyone on my team returned home safe.

THE PICTURE ON THE BOX

In a complex leadership situation – and most leadership situations are complex because they involve people – it's essential to know where we're heading. This is perhaps a statement of the blindingly obvious, but in my experience it's something often forgotten. Or, at the very least, it's taken for granted as something that everyone involved knows. I like to think of any leadership situation as a jigsaw puzzle, where the puzzle pieces are individual team members, their roles, and all the elements of the tasks involved in the project. Just like a jigsaw puzzle, unless we have a clear **picture on the box**, it's very difficult for the pieces to come together in a meaningful and effective way.

As leaders, it also falls to us to paint that picture. As with my talk to my team after the photo shoot in the desert, that picture needs to be simple, clear, and as vivid as possible, so that all can understand, regardless of their role or position. It needs to make sense to each and every person involved so that they have the opportunity to make it personal by seeing how they can play their part. When leaders provide this clarity, their team members can begin to figure out for themselves what they can do to help build that picture – to create that outcome. When the picture is clear enough, it can inspire those beyond our immediate team to support what we're trying to accomplish too.

A CLEAR PICTURE BUILDS MOMENTUM

Malala Yousafzai was only fifteen years old when she was shot by the Taliban on her way home from school in the Swat Valley, northwest Pakistan. Even at that age, Malala had been known as an activist, campaigning for all girls to receive an education – something that was not a given in her country, as in many other countries around the world. Her campaigning went against the beliefs of the Taliban organization and led to her attempted assassination in October 2012.

Remarkably, Malala survived. More than that, the experience strengthened her resolve. On her sixteenth birthday, just nine months after the attack, she spoke at the United Nations in New York. In simple words, she painted her compelling picture when she said, "One child, one teacher, one book and one pen can change the world." This became her rallying cry for a movement to champion twelve years of free, safe education for every girl in the world, regardless of their background. In 2014, in partnership with her father, Malala created the Malala Fund, whose mission it is to deliver on that picture of the future. Since then she has attracted support from individuals, companies, and foundations around the world, and has been able to invest over $22 million to help every girl to have the opportunity to learn and lead.

When we take a stand for something that is really important to us and use it to paint a clear picture of the future we want to create, it opens up the possibility for people who share that feeling to join us too. When that happens, momentum builds as others bring their energy, innovation, and drive, as they too begin to step up and lead.

While it is important to have a clear picture of the outcome or future we want to create, it's not enough on its own, particularly if that outcome involves stepping into the unknown – somewhere beyond our experience. We need to embrace a complete shift in mindset.

STANDING AT THE TOP OF THE MOUNTAIN

I love to run. I particularly love running in the wild countryside, across hills and mountains, with a pack of essential kit on my back. During my military service, I completed several survival courses in desolate areas of the world. There's a wonderful sense of freedom that comes from knowing how to take care of yourself in the wilderness. On reflection, this chimes well with my stand for being self-reliant.

Some years ago I decided I would complete a solo run up the three highest mountains in England, Scotland, and Wales.

I had run up the Welsh mountain, Snowdon, before, but the other two peaks – Scafell Pike and Ben Nevis – would be a new experience. To make it more interesting, I'd attempt to run up and down all three within a single 24-hour period. I'd have a trusted colleague – Graeme, who had served with me during the Iraq War – to drive me the considerable distance between the three hills. Importantly, Graeme would be my safety man, watching me out and back in from each run. He'd also ensure I had hot food ready to eat as we travelled to the next location.

Since this would be quite a challenge, I felt it would be worth using it to raise some money for charity. I chose two charities: one in support of cancer treatments, the other for research into Alzheimer's. Each of these diseases had affected one of my parents during their final few years of life, so supporting those charities added deeper meaning to my challenge, taking it beyond purely a personal physical feat.

On the day I achieved what I set out to do, finding my way through snow blizzards and gales, completing the run within the time limit. I also raised several thousand pounds for the charities.

While that was all personally very satisfying, I tell this story now because it helps illustrate how we can choose to think and lead when facing something we haven't done before. It's about drawing on the energy that's available to us when we emotionally connect to the future state we wish to bring into existence, rather than being held back by doubts or by the limitations of our past. It's what I call **standing at the top of the mountain**.

This is how it works.

Before I started each run, I would visualize what it would look like standing at the top of the mountain. I would imagine the contours of the summit – what I would be able to see from that height as the horizon stretched out in front of me. Importantly, I then took it a vital step further: I connected *emotionally* with how it *felt* as I stood at the top of that mountain. This emotional element is critical. I imagined the sting of the cold breeze on my skin, the freshness of the air in my lungs, and the relief in my legs after the effort. I connected to the feeling of exhilaration on reaching the top, as the cocktail of endorphins and other chemicals surged through my body. I visualized looking back down the mountain at the path I had chosen and thinking how good it felt to have overcome it. I thought about how it felt when I called Graeme on my radio to let him know I was safely at the top. Lastly, I imagined how satisfying it felt to have achieved the goal, to be able to return home, collect the sponsorship money, and hand it to the charities.

By the time I started running, in my mind I'd already reached the summit.

This is a very different mindset – a completely different world – from one where we are standing at the bottom of the mountain looking up at the daunting task ahead, thinking to ourselves that we'll give it our best shot. When we are standing at the bottom, all we can see are the obstacles and the tortuously steep path. Doubt then inevitably creeps in, particularly if we haven't done the task before.

If you want to run up a mountain, start at the top.

This is exactly how we need to lead when we are stepping into the unknown or contemplating a formidable task we haven't taken on before. It applies if we're literally running up a mountain, or leading in combat, launching a new company, achieving a project target, or being a great parent. Starting at the top of the mountain is not about arrogance. It is about harnessing the reservoir of energy we have inside of us to prevail even when, as Musk said, the odds are not in our favour. It's about leading with *commitment*.

COMMITMENT

When we make a **commitment**, we choose to create an unshakeable bond *with ourselves*. It's a choice to hold ourselves accountable to deliver.

Making a bond with ourselves goes beyond, say, signing any written contract. This is because without that solemn promise we've made to ourselves, when circumstances become difficult, we'll likely seek a way around any written contract. When we make a commitment with ourselves, we are saying we will deliver even if it means making sacrifices along the way. The energy and drive for a commitment again comes from a stand – something that is really important to us. Often we talk about commitments when actually they are just priorities – things we will do until something else we feel to be more important comes along. Priorities are fine, but they're not going to get us to the top of our mountain.

However, having a commitment and keeping it to ourselves is not enough either. We also need to *declare* it. In other words, we need to share our commitment by telling others. The act of verbally sharing adds weight to the promise we have made. It also gives other people the opportunity to support us, and to call us out if we waver!

Let's take the example of two people who, individually, make a New Year's resolution to give up smoking.

The first does so because, well, he just feels he should give it a go. After all, he reasons, it's a popular thing to do at the start of the year, and he's seen the campaigns on television. He keeps the resolution to himself, not mentioning it to anyone else.

The second person chooses to make a commitment to give up smoking because she wants to be able to run around with her kids more – something she's been struggling with lately. She also wants to be there for them later in life. It's based on her stand for being a good mother. She emotionally connects with what that looks like and feels like. She tells her friends, family, and work colleagues of the commitment she's made and why, asking them to help by calling her out if anything she says or does isn't in tune with that commitment.

Which person is more likely to give up smoking? I'd put my money on the second person every time.

The commitment Malala made when establishing her fund is based on her stand for girls' education. She's painted the picture of what that future looks like. The fund is her very public declaration of bringing that future to life.

The commitment Elon Musk has made to colonize Mars is declared through his company, SpaceX. It's based on his stand for the sustainability of the human race.

The commitment many of us declare when we choose to become parents, shown through the personal compromises we make such as the example of giving up smoking, is to give our kids the best possible opportunities in life with no expectation of anything in return.

In my case, I'd made a commitment to run up those three peaks. My stand for self-reliance certainly had a part to play. But the real powerhouse of energy came from my stand for helping others, the connection to my late parents, and not wanting to let others down. Asking people to sponsor me was a public declaration of my commitment. Despite the hazardous conditions, from the snow blizzard on top of Ben Nevis to the gales on top of Scafell Pike and Snowdon, the notion of not completing the challenge never once entered my head.

SHARED COMMITMENT

When we declare a commitment to achieve something, based on what is deeply important to us, we create an environment in which others have the opportunity to join with us in that commitment. When they can see clearly what we're collectively trying to achieve, people at all levels start to rise as leaders too. When we hit the hurdles along the way, as we inevitably shall, our view from the top of the mountain will give us the mindset we need to keep going and find our way through.

However, even when we embrace all of this, there will, at some point, be something waiting in the shadows.

Fear.

And that's what we'll take a look at in the next chapter.

—— CONSIDER THIS ——

When we can cut through the noise to focus on what really matters to us – as an individual and to our team – it brings clarity. This also acts as the foundation for painting a compelling picture of where we are committing to go – the top of our mountain. This becomes the catalyst for coordinated action.

◆ LEARNING TO FLY

Consider this: What are you committed to bringing about in your life?

Practise painting the picture of what it will look like when you get there, viscerally connecting with that feeling, and sharing the picture with others.

The next time you're working with others and something seems unclear, don't be afraid to ask for clarification – if you have the question, someone else likely does as well. Ask them to paint the clearest picture possible so everyone can be on the same page.

◆ FLYING

Consider this: Consistency of words and actions builds integrity and character.

If you are part of a team focused on accomplishing a project or outcome together, take the time to build a shared understanding of what that outcome will look like and feel like, and why it matters at a personal level. The clearer that picture is, the more momentum you will build to achieve it.

◆ TEACHING OTHERS TO FLY

Consider this: As you lead your team, take the opportunity to make the link between the actions you are taking as a team and how that relates to the shared commitment you have – the picture on the box.

Seek out opportunities to acknowledge how individuals contribute to the shared commitment, be they on the front line or in a support capacity. This will create an opportunity for them to commit to their individual pieces in a more meaningful way.

◆ LEADING FROM THE JUMPSEAT

Consider this: The next time your team is confronted with an obstacle or challenge, ask them how they want to handle it.

Encourage them to see it from the top of the mountain, rather than the potentially daunting view looking up from the bottom.

Support team members in their commitment to making it happen, even when they're stepping into the unknown.

Celebrate and acknowledge those who innovate, and show creativity in bringing this commitment to life.

Chapter 5

Fear in the Shadows

THE PRACTICE OF Jumpseat Leadership draws its strength from the commitments we choose to make. By their nature, commitments represent something we value deeply. They will not always be easy to uphold, especially when we're faced with conflicting priorities or short-term needs. This is when **fear** raises its head.

Fear is a powerful force. It's also an important one – fear can help keep us alive. Fear triggers the freeze, flight, or fight reaction, which was so vital in keeping us safe from wild animals or other dangers when we were all hunter-gatherers thousands of years ago. Thankfully, these days the vast majority of us do not have our lives threatened on a regular basis. And yet there are times when fear still grips us, such as when we hear a loved one has been in an accident, or a son wants to ride a powerful motorbike.

In our modern world, fear can be triggered when we sense our *livelihood* is in danger. If our job, business, or way of living comes under attack, fear can activate the same freeze, flight, or fight reaction our ancestors felt when they heard a rustle in the long grass. Suddenly discovering we're out of work, or when a competitor has taken customers away from our main product line, or if the open countryside next to our home is about to be developed into high-rise office blocks, will cause fear to raise its head. Or maybe we've stepped into the unknown and are several months into launching a new business, when suddenly doubt creeps in. We feel a flash of fear in the gut as we wonder if we've made the wrong choice or worry we're not up to the task. When SpaceX lost its third rocket in a row, Musk knew that the next launch had to succeed, otherwise it would be, in his words, "absolutely game over". Fear was lurking.

While our reaction in each of these situations will likely be less physical than when our life is in the balance, it is nonetheless very real. We might feel paralyzed with shock, want to run away from the situation, or retaliate by taking up a position against whatever it is that's threatening us. We're afraid of losing the livelihood that means so much to us, and we desperately want to hold on to what we have created.

Our fear can be equally real and even more immediate when we feel our *status* or *reputation* is being undermined. Perhaps we've been passed over for that promotion we so richly deserve. Or we feel misrepresented in the press, on social media, or in daily workplace gossip. Or maybe someone else has joined the company where we work and seems to be so much better at everything than we are. Or the trigger could be something as simple as when, during the morning rush hour, another driver barges their car ahead of ours in a line of traffic. All of these situations will cause us to react, as we feel our status or reputation within the hard-fought human hierarchy is being challenged or diminished. That reaction is being driven by fear, just like the fear I felt while driving to give my talk to the RAF.

Unfortunately, regardless of whether it's a threat to our life, livelihood, status, or reputation that is causing our survival instinct to kick in, fear is not always the most helpful reaction. It can cloud judgement, give us tunnel vision, or have us lash out inappropriately. We've all been there. It's human.

In its purest form, when we allow fear to drive us, it will occur as self-preservation. But fear will take on other forms too, including ego, self-doubt, self-pity, timidity, deflection, anger, or arrogance. We might seek to protect ourselves by closing down from others and hiding our feelings. Whatever form it takes, fear has a focus on *self first*. Fear is associated with a world defined by scarcity and positions, as we fight against the threat. It's the world of win or lose. After all, our instinct will tell us that, unless we survive as an individual, then there's no future.

THERE IS AN ALTERNATIVE

Fortunately, there's another equally powerful force we can channel. It's a force that has us driven by humble confidence. Instead of scarcity, we see possibility and abundance. This force can also appear as hope, mutual respect, humility, compassion, courtesy, or appropriate vulnerability. Whatever form it takes, this force is focused *outward* rather than inward – on *others first* instead of self first. Rather than taking a position against something, we take a stand for what really matters. We make a commitment.

This force is **love**.

Now, I'm conscious that, by mentioning the word "love", I may risk losing some of you reading this. Your immediate reaction might be to question how love can play a part in tough leadership situations or in everyday business life.

But hang on a minute.

The words I used to speak to my people before combat operations in the Iraq War came from love, not fear. I spoke of the need to do our job to protect the lives of those who depended on us. Our actions would be in service of others. Equally, my ability to sit calmly in the jumpseat, as Calum wrestled with the controls, came from love, not fear. I had absolute confidence in his ability to do what needed to be done. All I needed was the humility not to interfere, so he could do his job.

It's impossible to work towards becoming a Jumpseat Leader, focused on lifting others up, if we allow ourselves to be driven by fear. For one, our egos would get in the way if we feared the success of others. It would be like playing soccer with our kids and always having to be the one to score.

Being driven by fear limits what we can achieve. Fear puts the brakes on. In our world of scarcity, we become focused on protecting what we have, rather than seeing possibility and what could be. When facing a challenge or leading into the unknown, fear would never allow us to reach the top of that mountain. Instead, we would be blinded by all the obstacles along the path. As Descartes said, "We do not describe the world we see, we see the world we can describe." In other words, if we choose to see the world as a place of scarcity and despair, that will be our experience. If, however, we choose to see the world as a place of possibility and hope, that will be our experience instead.

Fear closes down. Love opens up. We get what we nurture.

Like light and darkness, fear still has an important role in the love–fear relationship. Fear is the catalyst for courage. Without fear, courage cannot exist. Courage is not about a lack of fear. In this context, courage is about recognizing fear as a warning flag and then choosing to be driven by *love for* something rather than *fear of* something. When we make that leap, love will sustain our courage and give us the energy to continue against the odds.

AGAINST THE ODDS

On the morning of 7th February 2007, Kath Doran, the managing director of Spectrum Plastics, received news that sent a surge of fear through the company's workforce. Based in Stockport, England, Spectrum's business was deceptively simple: to print and then encapsulate any paper or card in plastic. It's something we tend to take for granted – café menus, membership cards, posters – anything printed that needs to be weatherproof, wipeable, or hygienic. The call Kath Doran received that morning was from Spectrum's biggest client, a British catalogue-based retail store. Without any notice, they had just decided to end their contract with Spectrum and give it to another supplier. Worth £2.7 million, this work represented around 70 percent of Spectrum's annual revenue, and losing it could easily cause them to fold. By any measure, this was catastrophic news.

After joining Spectrum in 1988, at the age of 21, Kath had risen to become managing director in 2004, and she had led the company through highs and lows ever since. The company's history dated back to 1922, and Kath was now facing a challenge that threatened their continued existence. But the idea of giving up never passed through her mind. The approach she chose to take, however, would be critical to the outcome. She recognized that she could choose to be driven by the fear that was welling up inside her, looking inward, and taking steps to protect herself. Or she could find the courage to be driven by love, looking outward, and taking care of her team.

Acting on fear would likely have led to Kath making drastic cuts, maybe even threats to her employees, telling them they needed to find ways still to hit their targets or she would be pulling the plug. All of this would have been completely understandable from a business perspective and easy to rationalize. Few other company directors would have criticized her. These actions would also have protected Kath's own livelihood and status. While this approach may well have kept the company afloat in the short term, it would have devastated the trust, morale, and engagement of her team. Taking these fear-based measures may have been the easier choice, but Kath wasn't going to do any of that. She chose the other path, based on love. This is almost always a harder path to follow, since it often calls on self-sacrifice and increased emotional investment, all in service of others. But the outcome is almost always more rewarding. Fear has us step back; love has us step forward.

Kath felt a deep sense of responsibility for the livelihoods of all the people on her team. Many of them had mortgages to pay and families to sustain. She couldn't let them down. She also wanted to ensure Spectrum would be able to continue far into the future, even when she was no longer at the helm. That was her commitment, no matter how hard it would be.

Spectrum had prudently built up some cash reserves, and so Kath announced the company would use this to pay everyone until they had figured things out. "We are going to survive," she declared to her anxious team. She went a step further and also declared they would use the lull in business as an opportunity to figure out how they could do things better. Kath's words immediately reduced the fear across her workforce, while also opening up headspace for creativity and innovation.

Courage started to spread.

Kath's next step was to ask each of her experienced machine operators to measure the maximum sustainable production speed of their individual machines, over a period of several weeks, as they worked on their smaller contracts. This allowed them to assess production costs very accurately, which in turn helped them to offer more finely tuned bids for new work.

Kath also decided, despite her years of experience, that she needed to develop new skills herself, so she engaged advisers in finance and marketing. She knew each of them through the network she had created over the years, and now called them "The Board You Cannot Afford". She extended this thinking to her whole team, giving every individual employee the opportunity to take on nationally recognized training and development, covering everything from production management and IT to customer service and sales.

Kath's choice to be driven not by fear but by the love for her people, and the history of the company had a decisive effect. Six months after the news of the cancelled contract, she had limited their annual loss to £140,000. Twelve months later, when the 2008 recession hit, Spectrum was already prepared with the culture and attitude to help them weather the storm. Kath's commitment to her people was recognized too: a little over two years later, Spectrum won a national award for learning and development in the workplace.

Today the company is still going strong, while some others in the sector are no longer around, including the competitor who took over Spectrum's main contract in 2007.

WE'RE ALL HUMAN

It would be wonderful if we could all be perfect and always be driven by love. To be one of those people who always put others before themselves. Seeing possibility instead of scarcity. Taking a stand instead of a position. Showing humility and keeping our ego in check as we always do the right thing.

But let's get real. We're human.

Imagine you're driving and in danger of arriving late for an important work appointment. As you arrive at your destination, you dive into the nearest free parking space, pretending you didn't see the other driver who had been waiting to take that space. (Your livelihood is on the line if you miss that meeting. Fear takes over.)

Or you're at work and one of your team loses an important sale. You react by letting rip and chewing them out in front of the others. (Your livelihood, status, and reputation are all on the line if you don't make that team target. Fear takes over.)

Or your four-year-old kid accidentally knocks over their drink while you're having lunch together in a fancy restaurant. Perhaps you didn't get much sleep the previous night. You're immediately annoyed and embarrassed, reacting angrily and scolding them. (Your status or reputation as a parent with well-behaved children has been undermined. They should know how to behave better. Fear takes over.)

None of these events would likely make us proud if we were to reflect on them later. Indeed, we'd probably feel disappointed in ourselves or, alternatively, bluster through by robustly rationalizing what we did. But that's okay – no one gets it right all of the time.

This doesn't mean we should give ourselves a free pass to behave in ways we will later regret. But it does mean that, on occasion, we can cut ourselves some slack. The *trend* over time, of the way we choose to lead ourselves and others, is more important than each and every action. If that trend is more towards being guided by love drivers than fear drivers, it will open up greater possibilities for us as leaders. Not only will this trend shape our world, it will add to the foundation of our character and how others see us.

We need a technique to help minimize the times we react from fear.

REACT AND RESPOND

As a pilot, one of the alerts that really grabs your attention is the one that tells you there's an engine fire. On large passenger jets this alarm usually takes the form of a very loud bell, together with a big, red light to show you which engine is burning. The effect is dramatic. The flight deck of a large aircraft is usually a quiet and peaceful place. To have that shattered by the deafening noise of an engine fire alarm is a considerable jolt. Even when it occurs in a simulator, your heart skips a beat.

Before a pilot has been fully trained in handling these situations, it's natural for fear to take over. In an instant, your primeval instinct assesses the options: freeze, flight, or fight. Well, you can't run away – you're at 35,000 feet, so leaving now would really upset the passengers. There are no wild animals to fight either. So there's only one option left: you freeze. Paralysis sets in.

Clearly, if all we can do is freeze, this situation is unlikely to turn out well. This is why professional pilots train extensively to deal with these and other potentially heart-stopping emergencies. When an engine fire alarm sounds, the crew will carry out what are known as **immediate actions**. These are a short series of predetermined actions designed to handle the situation in the best way possible. Immediate actions are memorized so, as their name suggests, they can be correctly carried out without hesitation. Importantly, the first action is to cancel the noise of the bell. It's done its job. You now know there's an engine fire.

Immediate actions are an example of a **response** taking the place of what would otherwise be a **reaction**. Reactions tend to be instinctive. If we're reacting to something that is really important to us, our reaction will be driven by either fear or love. A fear reaction would have us step back from the warning sound of a rattlesnake, while a love reaction would have us step forward if the snake were threatening a young child.

A **response**, on the other hand, is different. It is more considered. Like immediate actions, a response is what we offer when we've had time to reflect on a given situation. The immediate actions for an aircraft engine fire have been carefully put together by experienced engineers and pilots, who have thought through the order of what needs to be done and when. Importantly, they've worked out this response sitting in comfortable offices, not while on aircraft engulfed in flames. Immediate actions allow a pilot to *respond* to a situation at the exact moment when a fear-based reaction would otherwise be more likely.

We can use the same approach in everyday leadership moments. If our intent is to lead without fear getting in our way, we can take the time to recognize when we might be triggered into an unhelpful fear-based reaction. When we can anticipate these moments, we can acknowledge fear as the warning flag, just like the engine fire bell. We can then respond in a way that is love-driven and generative.

This could be as simple as taking responsibility for being late to a meeting because you didn't allow enough time to find a parking space, rather than pretending that traffic was heavy. Or being curious about why your salesman lost the sale and asking how you might have supported them better. Or anticipating that your four-year-old might be so excited about visiting the fancy restaurant that they might knock something over, and deciding you're not going to let this spoil the family experience.

For all those times when we can't anticipate the actions of others and fear grabs us when we least expect it, we can also say, "I'll tell you my immediate reaction now. Tomorrow, when I've had time to reflect, I'll give you my considered response."

WE ALWAYS HAVE A CHOICE

As in the story of Kath earlier, we always have a choice of love over fear, of seeing challenges and opportunities instead of static problems. We even have that choice in the most extreme of circumstances.

After Malala Yousafzai had been shot, it would have been understandable for her to be driven by fear and withdraw. To shy away from those who oppose her and what she stands for. On the contrary, Malala chose love, embracing the problem of those who wanted to silence her. She addressed it as a challenge and created opportunity. In her own words from her speech to the United Nations a year after her attack:

> Dear friends, on 9 October 2012, the Taliban shot me on the left side of my forehead. They shot my friends, too. They thought that the bullets would silence us, but

they failed. And out of that silence came thousands of voices. The terrorists thought they would change my aims and stop my ambitions. But nothing changed in my life except this: weakness, fear and hopelessness died. Strength, power and courage was born.

I am the same Malala. My ambitions are the same. My hopes are the same. And my dreams are the same. Dear sisters and brothers, I am not against anyone. Neither am I here to speak in terms of personal revenge against the Taliban or any other terrorist group. I am here to speak for the right of education for every child. I want education for the sons and daughters of the Taliban and all the terrorists and extremists. I do not even hate the Talib who shot me.

This speech was driven by love. A stand for what she believes in. It's about the opportunity to lift others up – even the children of those who would have her dead.

In June 2018 I had the opportunity, through a mutual friend, to meet Malala, while she was studying for her degree at the University of Oxford. She kindly took us on a tour of her college, Lady Margaret Hall. As we walked and talked, I was especially taken aback by her quiet courage and humble confidence. Despite her worldwide recognition and numerous accolades, including the Nobel Peace Prize, I didn't sense a jot of ego or arrogance.

Love or fear. We always have a choice.

—— CONSIDER THIS ——

While fear is naturally triggered when we sense our life is in danger, it also occurs when we perceive our livelihood, status, or reputation being threatened. Learning to recognize fear as a warning flag and to respond from love is essential for creating an environment that is generative and builds leaders.

◆ LEARNING TO FLY

Consider this: Practise sourcing your actions from love drivers rather than fear drivers.

When facing a setback, remind yourself of the love drivers pulling you forward. This is your source of sustainable energy.

The next time you react from fear and lash out at someone, or make a choice you later regret, reflect on what you could have done differently. Then, if the situation warrants it, go back, acknowledge you were previously reacting, and respond in the way you wish you had.

◆ FLYING

Consider this: Recognize you won't always "get it right" when you're applying yourself or when you interact with others.

Clear up the consequences and reflect that it's the overall trend of your actions that will define you.

◆ TEACHING OTHERS TO FLY

Consider this: Identify scenarios where your team could be faced with a particular challenge or opportunity.

Take the time to identify, as a team, where the potential fear drivers will be. Then step through those scenarios so your team can work through any reaction and develop a considered response that can be used if and when those scenarios occur, in the same way that pilots learn immediate actions to follow in an emergency.

Make it a habit to watch out for moments when your team reacts from a place of fear. Seek to understand what's behind that choice and help them reframe it through the perspective of a *love for* something rather than the *fear of* something. This will help them to respond better in the future.

◆ LEADING FROM THE JUMPSEAT

Consider this: Take time to recognize that your greatest accomplishments have been driven by love rather than fear.

Be the champion for love-driven actions and ways of speaking (for example, expressing a stand for something rather than a position against).

The next time you're asked to recount "the good old days", be sure to include some times when you chose love over fear. Help others to understand what triggered you and that it took courage to choose to be driven by *love for* something rather than *fear of* something.

—— Chapter 6 ——

Guardian of Hope

THE LADY IN THE TOWER

AS WE DESCENDED to begin our approach, I glanced down for my first look at Sierra Leone's Freetown Lungi International Airport, on the west coast of Africa. I could make out the single runway, pointing northwest across the beaches towards the Atlantic Ocean. Everything looked peaceful. And then I spotted the mortar craters splattered across the airfield.

This was 2002. The country was emerging from almost eleven years of civil war, and the craters were some of the outward scars. Looking down at the surrounding area revealed several piles of rubble, which I figured used to be buildings, set amongst clumps of lush vegetation sprouting from the deep-red earth. Despite the riches of diamonds that lay beneath much of this nation's soil, there was clearly a lot of work still to be done before Sierra Leone would heal completely. As is often the case with valuable natural resources, control of those diamonds had been a factor in the war.

In March 1991 the Revolutionary United Front, or RUF, had started a campaign to overthrow the Sierra Leone government. What followed was over a decade of fighting, military coups, and civilian abuse, as the RUF first prevailed and was then pushed back, only for the cycle to repeat itself. A multinational African armed force had tried unsuccessfully to intervene and regain stability. Meanwhile, murder, mutilation, and mass rape of the population became commonplace. Families were often separated, or worse, several generations slaughtered. Children who were spared were frequently conscripted into the RUF and forced to fight. This was the human race at its ugliest.

In 1999 the international community stepped in. An accord between the RUF and the government was agreed upon and signed, leading to a cessation in the fighting. The United Nations sent in a peacekeeping force to monitor disarmament, but the situation started to deteriorate again. The UK military deployed into the country the following year, to evacuate foreign nationals and help stabilize the situation. This proved to be a turning point in the conflict and, by the end of 2000, the war was declared over. Although fighting had stopped, some British troops remained in Freetown, providing support for the government, while also helping to rebuild and train the national military. On this flight to Sierra Leone in 2002, my aircraft held the latest batch of soldiers to help with the training effort.

We touched down, and I manoeuvred our large jet around the debris strewn across the taxiway, coming to a stop on the parking area. As our troops disembarked, I knew we had a couple of hours on the ground before returning to the UK. So, with my crew taking care of refuelling, I decided to walk over to the air traffic control tower to say hello to the controllers I'd been speaking to on the radio during our approach.

The tower showed all the signs of war. Paint peeled from the once smartly whitewashed building. Machine-gun fire had left dozens of pockmarks across the external walls. Where there had previously been windows, there were now only open spaces, including up at the top of the tower where the controllers sat. I let myself in through a door, which was only just managing to stay on its hinges, and climbed the steep staircase leading to a pair of swing doors and into the control tower itself.

I was greeted by the broad smiles of two local men in their early thirties. Removing their controllers' headphones, they welcomed me warmly. We were the only aircraft arriving that day, and they seemed delighted by the distraction.

In the corner over to my left, I noticed an elderly lady sitting quietly on a chair, busily knitting. I assumed she was the mother of one of the controllers. She looked up as I said hello and then, seeing my uniform, immediately came over and hugged me tightly around my waist, with her face pressed hard against my chest. With tears in her eyes, she repeated over and over, "Thank you, thank you, thank you ...".

I admit, this was not something I had been expecting and, at first, I didn't really know what to make of it. But I realized later that she wasn't thanking *me*. She had recognized my British uniform and the Union Jack on my sleeve. After years of suffering devastation and atrocity in her country, she was acknowledging what that flag represented to her: hope. Through all this time, she had held on to the hope that the situation in her country would improve. The arrival of British troops wearing the same uniform as me fuelled her hope. She could start to see the possibility of stability and peace returning at last.

Like fear, hope is a powerful force. The difference is that hope is sourced from love – an enduring belief that there will be an "after", no matter how dire our current situation. Hope can be difficult to quantify, although we all know when we have it, as sure as we know when we don't. The presence or absence of hope in us can be seen by those around us too.

Jim Collins, in his book *Good to Great*, shares the story of United States Navy Vice Admiral James Stockdale, who spent eight years as a prisoner of war during the Vietnam War. Many of his men who were prisoners alongside him survived, while many others did not. Stockdale identified that the survivors were those who held on to hope – hope that one day they would be released. The prisoners who *didn't* survive were the optimists – those who believed they would be released by, say, Christmas or Easter. As these dates came and went, their optimism waned. Without hope they fell into despair and, as Stockdale put it, they died of a broken heart.

Optimism alone isn't enough. To endure, we need hope.

BASECAMP

To hold on to hope is to make a commitment. And yet hope cannot be disconnected from our current reality. Just as we have hope for the future, we need to acknowledge and embrace the present, no matter how daunting it is. The two must work in tandem. It's like when we set out to climb a mountain: we must first establish our **basecamp** and take stock of our people, equipment, and circumstances. We might have all the training and supplies we need, yet the weather means we're not going any further today. The lady in the tower who had endured years of conflict in Sierra Leone, and Stockdale and his men held prisoner, needed to accept that their situations were unlikely to change in the immediate future. Hope alone would not alter the circumstances over which they had no control, but hope *would* give them the strength they needed to survive until their circumstances changed.

Thankfully, most of us do not find ourselves in such extreme situations, where all we have left is hope. There is usually action we can take. However, we still need to hold on to hope, alongside recognizing the reality of our situation.

In the previous chapter, when Kath of Spectrum Plastics received the news of their cancelled contract, she needed to confront the reality of losing 70 percent of their annual revenue overnight, and of the very real danger it posed to the business. No amount of hope would have changed those facts. Fully recognizing their situation gave her the solid foundation she needed to build the options that would lead them out of the crisis. Equally, if Kath, as their leader, had lost hope for the future, those in her team would likely have lost hope too. They may have accepted their situation and yet not have had the hope to keep themselves going.

For highly technical and ambitious start-ups, it's even more vital for leaders to embrace both hope and reality. In the early days of SpaceX, Elon Musk needed to confront the reality of all the failed launches and methodically address what had caused them. Throughout, he continued to have hope – a staunch belief – that the company would, at some stage, see repeated success with their rockets. Keeping this hope alive is what will give everyone in SpaceX the stamina and resilience they need to eventually get people to Mars.

Whether we are dealing with a crisis, a business setback, or trying to bring a new product to market, as leaders we need to be guardians of hope, while also accepting the reality of our circumstances. In April 1970 hope and reality dramatically came together for all the world to see.

APOLLO 13

On 13th April 1970 the thirteenth Apollo mission, carrying three US astronauts to land on the moon, was suddenly faced with an emergency threatening the lives of all those on board. One of the oxygen tanks, in the section of the spacecraft known as the service module, ignited. The explosion caused the loss of all the oxygen from that part of the spacecraft – the main supply needed to generate electricity, using fuel cells, which would also keep the astronauts alive for the majority of their flight.

At the time of the explosion, Apollo 13 and its crew had already covered two thirds of their journey to the moon and were travelling away from the Earth at a speed of 25,000 mph. It quickly became clear to NASA's mission control in Houston that the astronauts had neither sufficient oxygen nor enough electrical power to return to Earth in the usual way, if at all. Their situation seemed hopeless.

Gene Kranz, the 32-year-old NASA flight director, was on shift at mission control at the time of the Apollo 13 explosion. It became Kranz's job to lead the team over the days that followed to get the astronauts home. Faced with a seemingly impossible challenge, Kranz was relentless in holding on to hope and inspiring the same in his team.

The first thing Kranz did was to embrace the reality they faced. That meant acknowledging their planned lunar landing was no longer possible – a tough call in itself, given the years of planning and millions of dollars it had taken. Their mission had changed now to one purely of survival and rescue.

The spacecraft had lost many critical systems, including life support, and they had to assess the impact of each of these. In the 1995 Universal Pictures movie *Apollo 13*, a scene depicts Kranz, played by Ed Harris, gathering his team of engineers and technicians together shortly after the explosion. He establishes his "basecamp", listening to each of his system specialists as they share the reality of what they are facing. The scene ends with Kranz declaring, "Failure is not an option!" While this exact phrase was a creation of Hollywood, it captured the attitude of Kranz and the whole NASA team whenever they faced challenges. Indeed, the real-life Kranz adopted that line for the title of his autobiography, since it so accurately reflected the leadership culture: hope coupled with reality.

WAREHOUSE OF POSSIBILITY

By embracing reality, being clear on their new mission, and sustaining hope, Kranz created what I call a **warehouse of possibility**.

Imagine a large warehouse. At the moment there is nothing inside. But what's important is this building represents a *possibility*. In Kranz's case, it was the possibility that all the astronauts could return home safely. Like a sign above the main warehouse door, this was Kranz's unshakeable commitment. It was a commitment born of his character – his stand for never giving up and taking on a challenge, no matter how difficult or daunting.

This warehouse of possibility is vital because it provides a space in which the possibility can grow. At first, a small office is likely to appear in one corner of the warehouse, with a sign on the door that says, "It can't be done". This is where the person lives who throws out all the reasons why getting the astronauts home safe is not going to happen.

We've all come across this person when taking on a new challenge. Their negativity can be quite irritating. However, their presence is also vital. They become the voice of the problems we face, giving us the opportunity to run towards the challenges and address them. If we're clear enough on the possibility we are committed to bringing about, it will inspire others to come to our warehouse and build their own offices inside. These new offices will have different signs above their doors, each representing a solution to one of the challenges we're facing.

In the case of Apollo 13, the technicians and specialists were inspired to work out how the equipment on board the space-craft could be used in different ways to get the astronauts home safely. The "offices" they created inside Kranz's ware-house of possibility represented the solutions for how to keep the crew breathing, how to conserve electrical power, how to use the gravity of the moon to slingshot the spacecraft back to Earth, how to navigate with the main computers turned off, how to correct the spacecraft's course so it entered Earth's atmosphere at the correct angle, how to stop the build-up of carbon monoxide from poisoning the crew .... The solutions came thick and fast. Eventually, the warehouse became full of all the solutions needed to get the crew back home. At that moment, the possibility turned into reality.

Apollo 13 splashed down safely in the South Pacific Ocean four days later on 17th April. The crew – Jim Lovell, Jack Swigert, and Fred Haise – all survived their ordeal.

In February 2016 I had the opportunity to chat over coffee with Lori Garver, while I was spending some time working with the US aerospace industry. In the late 1990s Garver served as NASA's assistant administrator – the second most senior role in the organization. While NASA has evolved since the race to the moon, Kranz's leadership remains a testament to what can be achieved when hope and possibility are kept alive. The Academy Award–winning movie by the same name, *Apollo 13*, is one of the best visual examples of all the ideas I've shared in this book so far, and of many of those I'll share in the chapters that follow. It's well worth a watch when you have the opportunity.

The lady in the tower in Sierra Leone wasn't trying to recover astronauts from a stricken spacecraft, nor did she have a formal team. But the reality she faced was an equally daunting story of survival. There was little that she could physically do, and yet she *could* hold on to the hope that her family and her country would get through what they faced. She created the space – her warehouse of possibility – into which others could step and help bring to life the future she imagined. Thankfully, she was still alive to see that happen. But even if she hadn't survived, I am convinced her quiet commitment to a better future would have lived on through those she left behind.

If we don't choose hope when facing overwhelming odds, we're already defeated.

The most important point about the warehouse of possibility is that it gives us, as leaders, a way to create the mindset where our team or others around us can become aligned and, together, cause something to happen. The warehouse of possibility is the vessel where hope can thrive. When Kranz made a commitment to bring all the astronauts home safely, and declared it to his team, everyone had the opportunity to contribute their part of the solution. Even when we have done all we can and there's still a chance of failure, hope is what keeps us moving forward.

In the final stages of the *Apollo 13* movie, when there is nothing else for them to do but wait for the re-entry and splashdown of the capsule, Kranz's character announces "I believe this is going to be our finest hour".

He was probably right.

HOPE AND POSSIBILITY

While facilitating a workshop for Nike in their Milan head-quarters, I was struck by the remarkable meeting space we were using. What made it remarkable were the eye-catching, poster-sized photographs on the walls.

On one side there were pictures of great and famous athletes, such as football player Cristiano Ronaldo, runner Mo Farah, basketball player LeBron James, and golfer Tiger Woods. On the opposite wall were photographs of the same size and prominence, only these were of unknown local athletes, who had yet to grow into their full potential. Together, these images captured hope and possibility. They embodied what really matters to Nike as an organization and what flows through all the people I've met there – they celebrate human achieve-ment, and by doing so, they inspire and energize others to go on and achieve more than they might have imagined. Along the way, they help keep people's hope alive, even in the face of inevitable setbacks.

Sometimes a warehouse of possibility could manifest itself as a single photograph, capturing how we'll feel when we achieve what we've committed to. Or, as Nike might say, that ware-house of possibility starts from simply putting on the right pair of shoes.

FULL CIRCLE

I had not thought about my flight to Sierra Leone and the lady in the tower for many years, until one chilly day in Frankfurt.

I'd just landed from London to give a keynote talk at the annual conference of a large consulting company. I was met in the baggage hall by a smartly dressed, quite distinguished-looking gent by the name of Ralph. He announced he would be my driver to take me downtown to my hotel.

Seated in the quiet of the immaculate Mercedes, I started to chat to Ralph. With his wispy, grey hair, I figured he was quite a few years older than me, and I was curious about how he came to be driving limousines for a living. As with the majority of Germans I've met, his English was perfect, so our conversation flowed easily.

It turned out Ralph owned the limousine company and simply enjoyed the driving and sense of freedom it gave him. It wasn't the first organization he'd run. In the 1980s and 1990s he'd had an export business, shipping and installing medical equipment to new hospitals in Africa.

"Which countries in Africa?" I asked.

"Oh, central and west Africa – a lot in Sierra Leone," came his reply. "Or at least until the civil war put an end to business. Do you know the region?"

My memory flashed back to the mortar craters, the shot-up air traffic control tower, and the lady hugging me. I told Ralph about my fleeting visit to Freetown airport and asked if he'd managed to get out of the country before the war. He said he'd stayed at first because, understandably, there was quite a demand for his medical equipment. When things had begun to get really dangerous, with foreign nationals also being shot, he had managed to catch one of the last flights back to Germany.

And then, a year later, with the fighting and atrocities at their height, he went back.

By this time we had reached my hotel, but I had to know more. Why on earth would he choose to go back to Freetown in the middle of the war? Ralph explained he'd made many friends during his time in Sierra Leone. Once he was back in Germany, he'd stayed in touch with as many of his contacts as he could, since he'd got to know their families and had frequently stayed at their homes. But the news then became increasingly disturbing.

Ralph had grown close to one family in particular – a business contact and his wife, their two young children, and their parents, all of whom lived in the same house in Freetown. Messages from them became less and less frequent, before stopping altogether. After many calls, he discovered to his horror that his business friend, his friend's wife, and their parents had all been slaughtered. And no one seemed to know what had become of the two young children.

Ralph knew he had to do something. He managed to get a flight into Freetown and, with the support of others, started to look for the children. After days of searching, and against all the odds, he found them and got them to safety.

"Where are they now?" I asked.

"Well," explained Ralph quietly, "I brought them back to Germany, and my wife and I raised them as our own. One of them is just finishing her degree at Edinburgh University, while the other has recently started work in finance here in Frankfurt."

Extraordinary leadership is to be found all around us, if we care to look. What emerged from my conversation with Ralph was what he stood for in life. He showed his ability to turn those stands into commitments and to act on them. He used fear as a catalyst for courage and was driven by the love for others. He held on to hope while dealing with the stark reality of what faced him. He has continued to lift up those children he rescued, who now seem to be thriving.

Did he need to do any of this? No.

Would anything have stopped him? Probably nothing on this earth.

When something is important enough to us, it becomes a *stand* and forms part of our character. Our stands act as a large reservoir of energy, which we can use to power the *commitments* we make.

As leaders, we need to foster the ability to *cut through the noise*, to capture the simple message – the mission, vision, or focus of what we are setting out to do. We ourselves need to connect to that focus at a personal level, and give those in our team the opportunity to make it personal too.

When fear raises its head, we need to recognize it as the warning it is, tempering our reaction and choosing instead to *respond* from *love*.

We need to also embrace *reality*, while remaining the guardians of *hope* – a belief that we will accomplish what we set out to do.

While we won't always get it right, when we intentionally put these ideas into practice, it builds the foundation of a culture where our people begin to step up and lead too.

We get what we nurture.

—— CONSIDER THIS ——

Whether leading ourselves or a team, we need to be able to embrace both hope and our current reality. Hope – a belief in something "after" – fuels our resilience and determination to move towards the world we imagine.

◆ **LEARNING TO FLY**

Consider this: The next time you're confronted with a seemingly impossible challenge, visualize what it looks like *after* you've conquered it.

Make a link back to your underlying commitment, sourced from the *love for* something.

Draw your energy from this picture, holding on to the belief that you will prevail, regardless of the setbacks you may encounter along the way.

◆ FLYING

Consider this: The next time you're given an assignment, look at it as a warehouse of possibility.

Name the outcome and hang the sign over the door so that others can choose to come and help you achieve it.

Encourage a naysayer to join you – they will help identify the challenges you will need to overcome.

◆ TEACHING OTHERS TO FLY

Consider this: Focus on framing the possibility you see for your team, your unswerving commitment to the outcome you're seeking – even when you're not sure how to get there – and holding the space, so that others may step up and contribute.

If your team is deep into a project and becomes focused solely on what is in front of them, take the time to have them step back and reconnect with the possibility you're working towards and why it matters at a human level. This will help to re-energize and further build momentum.

◆ LEADING FROM THE JUMPSEAT

Consider this: Seek opportunities to give verbal support, encouragement, and public acknowledgement to your senior people when they are the champions of hope, while also addressing the reality of the situation.

When necessary, be their confidant, partner, or sounding board, to help replenish their hope during particularly tough times.

Share your own experiences of when you've chosen hope in spite of the odds. Help them to apply that experience to their current reality so they can make their own choices to be guardians of hope.

HUMBLE
—— CONFIDENCE ——

──── Chapter 7 ────

Antidote to Ego

IT WAS 16TH FEBRUARY 1988, just a few days before my 25th birthday. I was the pilot for our military flight from the UK to Nairobi, Kenya. We had 130 troops on board, heading down for a stretch of training in the heat of the African bush, a trip we did quite regularly. We were always scheduled to fly through the night, to land just after the airport opened. It was often a visually dramatic approach, the sun rising through the early morning mist as we descended over Mount Suswa Conservancy park to the northwest of Nairobi.

Since you've read this far, you can probably guess what's coming next: today's approach was destined to become rather more dramatic than usual.

I was flying the aircraft and managing the flight. Meanwhile, the captain – the person in overall charge – liaised with air traffic control on the radios, obtained weather reports, and generally supported me. We'd then swap roles on the flight back to the UK. It's standard procedure on large passenger jets for the pilots to take turns in this way, as it gives each the opportunity to do the fun bit of having their hands on the controls.

At about eight miles from touchdown, I could see the runway straight ahead of us as we settled onto the final part of our approach. "Undercarriage down; landing checks," I ordered – the cue for the captain to operate a lever to lower the aircraft wheels and for us to run through the final checks before touching down.

As the captain moved the lever, three small, red lights appeared on the panel just in front of me, one each for the sets of wheels under either wing and one for the nose. It was completely normal for these lights to be red, before changing to green after about 30 seconds when the wheels were locked in the landing position. Only this time the light associated with the wheels under the left wing didn't change. It remained red.

I felt a momentary flash of fear surge through me. Not being able to get any of the wheels down for landing is not good in any aircraft, particularly a large passenger jet with over a hundred people on board. Without that set of wheels down, we would be faced with a crash-landing, with the likelihood of fire and people getting hurt as they evacuated the aircraft.

Fortunately, we have a checklist drill – a series of actions – to follow for this exceptionally rare event, which enables us to respond appropriately. The drill helps to quench the fear. It starts with selecting the wheels up and then selecting them down again. It's a bit like turning your computer off and then back on, and it usually solves the issue.

Still a red light.

It was clearly going to take longer to sort out the problem on this occasion, so we climbed away to a safe height and started to fly a holding pattern, well above the ground and away from other aircraft. We told air traffic control what was happening, and Tony, the captain, took control of the situation. He spoke to the passengers to let them know we had a small technical issue to resolve and, while we did that, the cabin crew would offer another (non-alcoholic) drinks service.

WORKING ON THE PROBLEM

We started to methodically work on the problem. As well as the two pilots, as part of our crew on our flight deck we also had a navigator and an air engineer, both highly experienced aviators who were trained to help in this situation. There were several levels of actions to go through, each of which should have resulted in the wheels coming down. None of them worked. Then there was the final drill, which never failed: we could manually winch the wheels down. Now, this might conjure an image of Tom Cruise climbing outside the aircraft, his face blasted by the slipstream, as he hangs off the wing while winding the wheel down by hand. Exciting though this might be, the reality is not quite like the movies, or at least not on our plane. There's a hatch in the floor next to the flight deck, which leads to a small area a bit like a cargo hold. Once inside, there are levers that can be used in an emergency to release each wheel from where it's retracted and stowed during flight, and then winched into the landing position. So that's what we did.

Only that didn't work either.

Unknown to us at the time, a printing error in a maintenance manual meant the cable between the lever and the wheels had not been properly connected. Just like a kite's broken string, the cable was never going to operate as it should.

Over the next two hours we tried everything we could, including rocking the wings and inducing what would have felt like turbulence to the passengers, trying to shake the wheels from their locked-up position. The red light remained stubbornly on. We were getting low on fuel and realized we had only one more option. We would need to crash-land.

As you might imagine, our passengers didn't greet this news with much enthusiasm. By now they had hoped to be settling into their barracks, enjoying a meal and a beer. Instead, they found themselves paying very close attention to the cabin crew, who were briefing them on what they needed to do to prepare for the crash-landing and evacuation. Although very similar to the standard instructions given before every flight, the safety briefing now quickly took on a greater sense of relevance and urgency. The passengers gave the cabin crew their undivided attention.

On the flight deck, it was fair to say we also weren't thrilled at the prospect of crash-landing. This aircraft had a long and unblemished safety record. As well as the threat to many lives, we would be potentially destroying a plane – one that was currently flying perfectly well. Similar to choosing to crash your car into a brick wall, the aircraft would actually be fine until the moment came for us to put it on the ground without one of its wheels down.

How we treat one another in these critical situations is telling. As the inevitability of what we faced became clear, there was no bluster of egos. Instead, there was openness, mutual support, and respect. We racked our brains to make sure we hadn't missed anything. We hadn't.

By now all of the early-morning flights had landed, with most being aware of our emergency. As the last British Airways flight taxied off the runway to head for its parking gate, its captain wished us the best of luck before leaving our radio frequency. Everything was suddenly quiet. We felt very alone.

With the cabin and passengers prepared, it was time to make our approach to crash-land on the runway. We could see all the fire trucks and emergency vehicles waiting for us, with those manning them no doubt also apprehensive of what was about to happen.

This is when the captain, Tony, turned to me and said calmly, "Peter, I want you to fly the approach and crash-land."

This is not something I'd been expecting. In times of emergency, it's usual for the captain to take control and fly the aircraft, just as Captain Sully did during the Miracle on the Hudson. It would be easy to assume that Tony had abdicated his responsibility, but that wasn't the case at all. Whatever choices he made, we were all in this together.

Looking back, his request to me made sense. Here's why.

Tony had several aspects to weigh up. He knew he was a very experienced and capable captain. However, he also knew that, while perfectly well trained and qualified in all the emergency procedures, he didn't have much experience flying this particular type of jet. He recognized that I, on the other hand, had thousands of flight hours on this aircraft. Significantly, having been assessed as having ability well above the average, I was also one of the very few pilots selected to fly the British prime minister around the world on state visits. Another factor was pure coincidence yet relevant: I'd recently completed a routine simulator flight practising this specific emergency. On balance, Tony decided it made better sense to have me handle the aircraft, while he focused on giving me the support I needed.

WHEN EGO STEPS FORWARD

This particular story is not about me, though. It's about Tony and what it took for him to ask me to carry out the crash-landing. He would no doubt have felt pressure to retain control and fly the approach. After all, he was the captain – he was in charge. Like the rest of the crew, he too would have been suppressing a degree of fear. Whenever you're in a position of authority, fear can generate a specific driver. That driver is **ego**.

Remember, fear emerges when we feel our life, livelihood, status, or reputation is threatened. It's a natural reaction. Above Nairobi airport, all of these were on the table for Tony.

What's important is what he chose to do about it. It would have been perfectly understandable for him to have reacted to that fear by allowing ego to take control. Ego easily could have told him, *You can do this*, or *You're the captain, you're the best person for the job*, when deep down, he knew there was a better option. Equally, ego might have prevented Tony from making his request of me, afraid that lifting me up and giving me the opportunity to excel might have taken away from his own status and reputation.

Whether ego shows up as loud and forceful or withdrawn and self-preserving, when it takes control, it can adversely affect our decisions. We start to *rationalize*, accepting or rejecting any input on the basis of whether it fits our story of self first. Strangely, the more we rationalize, the less rational we become.

There are other consequences too. When we're driven by ego, it gets in the way of progress. Those on the team soon sense it's only about us and no one else, and they begin to withdraw their support. We may not notice it at first, but discretionary effort – when people choose to do more than they are required to do – diminishes. When the leader or anyone on a team is driven by ego, it stifles innovation and ideas.

Ego has no place in Jumpseat Leadership. Nor, for that matter, in any healthy relationship.

ANTIDOTE TO EGO

There is an **antidote to ego**. It comes from the *love for* something – something that extends beyond just ourselves.

When we draw on this, it has us set aside thoughts that are self-serving. Instead, we choose to serve others.

In this case, Tony's antidote to ego was his commitment to the safety of all those on board. In the crucial moment, he judged that the best chance we had of surviving the crash-landing was to give control to his copilot and support him in every way he could. As with every shift from fear to love, that took courage.

However, letting go of ego does not mean we become timid and fade away. On the contrary, we still have a leadership role. What's different is how we show up. If Tony had become faint-hearted or hesitant in his decision making, it would have negatively affected the rest of the crew and our belief in our ability to take on the challenge. Because our captain acknowledged fear as a warning flag, he suppressed ego and chose instead to lead with **humble confidence**.

Having humble confidence meant Tony was appropriately resolute and focused, balanced with the willingness to listen and engage with other crew members. He created an environment where others felt they could offer ideas and contribute, rather than giving the impression he had all the answers. When, as a crew, we had explored all options and the time had come to make a decision, Tony did so without hesitation. In lifting me, his copilot, up, he also elevated the respect the crew had of *him* as a captain. We all knew he had made his decision based not on what fed his own status but instead on what was in the best interests of everyone on board. We all recognized the courage that took.

And what of the crash-landing? I flew the approach then, with less than a minute to impact, we heard a clunk that resonated throughout the aircraft. On the panel in front of me, the red light turned to green. All our wheels were locked down.

To this day no one knows how this happened, but I embraced it with open arms and made one of my smoothest touchdowns ever.

WHEN EGO GETS IN THE WAY

The emergence of ego is, of course, not constrained to the flight deck of an aeroplane.

In the first few days of 2018, I was running a workshop for the senior leadership team of one of the largest companies in the world, which had several very large divisions. The business was going through some significant challenges. Their longstanding presence in the marketplace had lost its sparkle, and over the past year their stock price had dropped more than 41 percent. If they were going to create a more promising future, they would need to do things differently.

For this workshop we had brought together the CEO and every divisional director. From the outset of the session, I could see from the dynamics in the room that fear was thinly veiled and ego was the dominant driver. Even before we started, most of the directors were trading remarks aimed at putting others down. One or two chose to step back and remain quiet, presumably hoping to stay out of the firing line. There was no willingness to confront and take ownership of where they were as a company. This was very much about the directors blaming each other.

The only person in the group who didn't seem to have ego at the forefront was the CEO. But there wasn't any sign of humble confidence from him either. In fact, he seemed to fade into the background, apparently content to allow the bickering between his people to dominate, rather than stepping in to close it down.

Humble confidence is built on a foundation of commitment. Commitment can only occur when it comes from our stands – from what we hold as really important. Stands become vital when we are dealing with the unknown or a crisis. As the workshop progressed, it became obvious to me that, whatever personal stands he had, the CEO wasn't drawing on them to guide his leadership. He was rudderless and drifting, able to react only from fear. As if to confirm my assessment, halfway through the workshop we had to adjourn for 90 minutes while the CEO and a few others dealt with a public relations crisis.

The big problem with ego is that it can quickly become infectious. If one person chooses to bluster with ego, others in the group often feel the need to do so too. Unless checked, herd mentality takes hold. Those who don't join in can become sidelined, their voices not heard and their ideas not shared. The long-term collateral damage to any team can be devastating. Ego can be expensive.

All this was happening right in front of me.

During the workshop, I created an opportunity for the directors to come together, to make a shift, and commit to something greater than themselves. The opportunity gave them the choice to use their fear as a catalyst for courage and reconnect to the love of what the company stood for and the difference it made in the world. If they had taken it, humble confidence would have started to emerge, guiding them out of their crisis. It could have been the start of a turning point. Sadly, they chose instead to continue the culture of fear, dominated by ego and blame.

We get what we nurture. Over the following twelve months, the company's stock price tumbled another 62 percent. The CEO was unanimously voted out by the other directors and resigned. As of August 2021, neither their standing as a company nor their stock price has recovered.

Now, if you're reading this and thinking, *I'm not a CEO so this is all very interesting but doesn't apply to me*, just pause for a moment before you skip ahead.

Leadership is available to us all. Regardless of our role, rank, or position on a team, at any time we can each choose to step up, set aside ego, and take responsibility. Imagine for a moment if the loudest person in that workshop had chosen to use their voice to take responsibility for their corporate situation, to show up with humble confidence. Or if the quietest person in the room had drawn on their stands to find the courage to speak up and stop the bickering. Indeed, when based on a stand, the quietest voice in a room can be the most powerful. A single director willing to make an intervention could have turned the tide of the conversation and created the space for an entirely different future to emerge – one in which every-one could start to contribute. This was not solely down to the CEO.

Would you have had the humble confidence to overcome ego?

WHEN EGO CAUSES DISASTER

At its worst, when ego grabs us, the consequences can extend way beyond a plummeting stock price. Perhaps one of the most notorious examples of this is when one person's ego, and the environment it created, cost the lives of 583 people, in an incident that became the deadliest aviation disaster of all time.

On 27th March 1977 dense clouds drifted over the runway of Los Rodeos Airport in Tenerife, the largest of the Spanish Canary Islands, off the west coast of Africa. Tenerife is a popular destination for those seeking some winter sun, and this was a busy time of the year, with both scheduled and charter flights converging on the archipelago. The main hub was Gran Canaria Airport, but this had been closed earlier that day because of a terrorist bomb attack on the terminal. Consequently, many flights had been diverted to a neighbouring island and into the small – and by now very congested – Los Rodeos Airport, known these days as Tenerife Norte Airport. Two of the diverted aircraft were Pan Am Flight 1736 from New York and KLM Flight 4805 from Amsterdam – both jumbo jets. Although only a 30-minute flight from one airport to the other, by ferry the journey takes five hours.

After a few hours, the Spanish authorities were able to secure the terminal at Gran Canaria and reopen the airport. Crews of all the diverted flights would have been eager to fly their passengers the short hop over to this, their original destination. Among them, refuelled and ready to go, was KLM Flight 4805, and the jumbo jet taxied to the runway for take-off. With so many planes on the ground and only one taxiway, in order to avoid gridlock, air traffic control had to instruct several jets to taxi down the runway before turning off.

The weather at Los Rodeos can change quickly. By the time KLM Flight 4805 reached the end of the runway, fog had descended over the airport. The KLM crew and air traffic controllers in the tower could no longer see each other. They also could not see Pan Am Flight 1736, which was still taxiing on the runway.

The KLM crew mistook a garbled radio message for clearance to depart and started their take-off run. They hit the Pan Am aircraft about halfway down the runway. The collision and subsequent fireball killed all the passengers and the entire crew aboard the KLM flight, as well as the vast majority of those on the Pan Am aircraft.

So why did this happen?

As Patrick Smith writes in his book *Cockpit Confidential*, many factors contributed to the accident, including the fog, the air traffic control tower not being able to see the aircraft, and poor radio procedures. However, the primary cause was found to be the KLM captain's decision to take off without proper clearance.

The captain of the KLM crew was Jacob van Zanten. An experienced pilot, at the time of the accident van Zanten was the chief flight instructor for KLM and head of the Dutch company's flight training school. As well as being recognized within the company as an expert on the Boeing 747 jumbo jet, he was also the "face of KLM", with his image appearing as part of an advertising campaign for the airline.

The radio and cockpit voice-recorder transcripts show that, after the KLM flight had started its unauthorized take-off roll, air traffic control instructed the Pan Am crew to report when they had cleared the runway. They responded, "OK, will report when we're clear."

The KLM flight engineer heard this on the radio and asked his pilots, "Is he not clear, that Pan American?"

Van Zanten replied, "Oh, yes," and continued the take-off.

The first officer, Klaas Meurs, did not challenge the captain's decision to go, and van Zanten did not listen to the flight engineer's tentative intervention either. As the most senior instructor captain at KLM, van Zanten enjoyed an almost celebrity status in the company, and it's unlikely the other crew members felt able to intervene more assertively. Van Zanten's ego was in charge. He knew best. If he'd been guided by humble confidence instead, it's likely he would have listened to those around him and others would have felt able to speak up. Van Zanten's status and ego, as it turned out, was a lethal combination.

The reason I know this story well is because of perhaps the only positive outcome from this tragic accident: the Tenerife disaster contributed to an important evolution of professional pilot training. Since the 1990s, every commercial and military pilot now receives instruction on what is known as crew resource management, or CRM.

CRM focuses on communication, decision making, and leadership in the cockpit. One aspect of the training is to ensure that even the most junior copilot has the confidence to question the actions of the most senior captain if they see or sense something is wrong. Pioneered by a former RAF pilot, David Beaty, the approach was adopted by United Airlines in 1981 and is now commonplace across the globe.

When I was a senior captain, I also held a high rank in my organization and fully recognized how this could adversely affect a junior copilot's willingness to speak up when we were flying. So, before every flight with a new pilot, I would remind them that their job was to monitor me carefully and to call me out if they thought I'd made a mistake or had missed anything. By giving them this permission, it not only promoted best practice, it also raised the game for the copilot, and encouraged their contribution. In other words, it lifted them up.

BUT WHAT ABOUT *TOP GUN*?

Some of you reading this might recall how fighter pilots were depicted in the 1986 Hollywood movie, *Top Gun*, starring Tom Cruise. Ego seemed to be a part of the fighter-pilot psyche. It makes for a good action movie, but while fighter pilots need to have belief in their ability, the reality is that this belief stops well short of unconstrained ego.

Naturally, when I was in military flying training, there was the occasional trainee whose ego seemed to be so great it entered the room before they did. These were the type who tended not to progress so well. Flying in formation with other jets to achieve a mission requires the highest level of teamwork. It's not a solo game.

In my experience, the best fighter pilots – the ones I trusted to have my back and would want to fly with – had left ego behind and led with humble confidence. They also tended to be the ones who survived a long career in what could be a dangerous role.

LETTING GO OF EGO

At the root of our journey to Jumpseat Leadership is the intent to lift others up so they may grow and take the lead. The aim is to equip them so we can eventually hand over the reins and take a step back. We can only do this if we are prepared to let go of our ego and lead instead with humble confidence. The sooner we do that, the greater the progress we will also make as a team or organization.

If we choose *not* to let go of ego, it will eventually get in the way by stifling innovation and engagement of those around us. When faced with the ego of a leader or of someone else on the team, people will either withdraw their contribution, as occurred dramatically on KLM Flight 4805; or they will lead with unconstructive confrontation and blame, as with the directors of the global company that had the tumbling stock price.

Either way, performance will suffer, people will become disenchanted, and when the moment is right, they will leave. In extreme situations, people can pay the ultimate price.

The challenge to let go of ego in a work environment becomes greater as we gain more expertise and experience in our chosen field. Ego can easily be triggered when we feel our status, or the reputation we've worked hard to achieve, is being threatened. We've all been there – the reaction seems to rise from our stomach, especially when someone challenges our authority, knowledge, or capability. This will cause opportunities to be missed or simply not even to materialize.

Key here is to acknowledge that the feeling comes from fear, and to have the courage to reconnect to something that goes beyond self. The surefire way to do this is to focus on lifting others up in service of a greater cause, just as Tony did during our approach to Nairobi airport, when we all needed to get safely onto the ground. To do this effectively calls on us to have humble confidence.

Ego – its presence or absence – is one vital aspect of how others see us as leaders and as people. Whatever is driving us from the inside, and how we come across – how we occur – to those on our team or around us, can be very different indeed. This is an aspect of leadership I haven't always got right, as you will read in the next chapter.

—— CONSIDER THIS ——

Whatever our stage of career or life, ego can raise its head and distort the way we lead. Practising humble confidence helps keep ego in its place.

◆ **LEARNING TO FLY**

Consider this: Recognize that ego can creep in when we least expect it.

Guard against this by ensuring you're not allowing fear to dominate, that you remain in service of something greater than yourself, and that you continue to listen to those around you.

The next time you feel threatened, pause before reacting and take a moment to identify where the fear is coming from. Are they really challenging you, or are they trying to contribute? What would happen if you chose to lift them up?

◆ **FLYING**

Consider this: Notice when over-confidence in your own ability is preventing you from hearing input from others.

Remind yourself there is always something to learn, even when you think you know how things are done.

The next time you're in a meeting and start to feel tensions rise, take the risk and disrupt the herd mentality before it starts. Rearticulate the stand that you all share and, if needed, help everyone see how each of their individual viewpoints reinforces that stand.

◆ TEACHING OTHERS TO FLY

Consider this: Be aware that your seniority and experience might make others reticent to suggest a different approach.

Encourage a continuous learning environment – one that includes you.

The next time you're working with your team to get a project across the line, challenge yourself to be the example of humble confidence. Create the environment for others to be able to contribute their ideas as you go through the decision-making process.

◆ LEADING FROM THE JUMPSEAT

Consider this: You should be used to recognizing when you can get hijacked by ego.

As you increasingly hand over the lead to others, recognize also that your ego can still flare up and take over, especially when something occurs that threatens your reputation. That is the time to ensure you remain driven by humble confidence.

The next time you're asked to take the lead on something, look to see who else could benefit from the opportunity, and suggest they take the lead instead. Then do everything in your power to support and lift them up as they take on the challenge.

Chapter 8

The Way We Occur

ONE OF THE greatest honours as a Royal Air Force officer is to be given command of a flying squadron. It's not only the people in your care that make this special. This is also about the history, the sacrifice, and the legacy of all those who have gone before you.

A squadron is the fighting unit of the air force. While the exact make-up will depend on the squadron's role, it can comprise up to several hundred personnel, including pilots, other specialist aircrew, maintenance engineers, and administrative support. A squadron commander will also have in their care aircraft, buildings, and additional facilities, some of which may be shared with other squadrons.

I remember as a young officer looking at the smart, highly varnished wooden plaque hanging on the wall of 101 Squadron headquarters. In carefully arranged gold lettering, it listed all the commanding officers of the squadron since the unit had been formed, on 12th July 1917, as part of the Royal Flying Corps, the precursor to the Royal Air Force.

The first individual on that list was the rather splendidly named Major The Honourable Laurence John Evelyn Twisleton-Wykeham-Fiennes. Born in 1890, he was the third son of Geoffrey Cecil Twisleton-Wykeham-Fiennes, the 18th Baron Saye and Sele. As such, he was a peer of the realm and part of ancient English nobility.

Broughton Castle, complete with moat and gatehouse, was built in 1300 and remains the family home to this day. Think *Downton Abbey* and you won't be far off. Contemporary members of this family include Sir Ranulph Fiennes, the renowned British explorer, and Ralph Fiennes, the Academy Award–winning actor, both of whom tend to use these abbreviated versions of their names, presumably to save time and ink.

As I looked up at the same plaque on Monday, 23rd July 2001, I now also saw my name. On the previous Friday, I had become the 55th commanding officer of the squadron. This felt both exhilarating and a little daunting – I was only too aware of the accomplishments of those who had gone before me. The squadron had lost many brave young souls during the battles of the two world wars. Indeed, because of its particularly hazardous role of jamming enemy radios during World War II, the squadron holds the distinction of having had the greatest number of casualties of any RAF unit during that conflict. The squadron motto, *mens agitat molem*, which translates as *mind over matter*, is more than a nod to what it would have taken to keep going amidst the tragedy of such loss.

Now it was my turn to be at the helm for the unit's next chapter. On that morning, little did I know that two years later I would be leading the current cadre of young men and women back into the fray to play their part in the Iraq War. But on that day in 2001, I had a more immediate concern occupying my mind: my first address to all squadron personnel since taking over from my predecessor. Indeed, at that moment, they were gathering expectantly in the briefing room next door.

A BIG MISTAKE

As I ordered my thoughts on what to include in my address, something else was bothering me. I couldn't get the image out of my mind of the man I'd succeeded, Ian, who had commanded the squadron brilliantly for the past two and a half years. Ian was an exceptional aviator and had led the squadron with distinction during the recent Kosovo conflict, for which he had been awarded the Order of the British Empire by Her Majesty The Queen. An accomplished raconteur, he was also the life and soul of any party. Everyone had the utmost respect for Ian. He seemed to tick all the boxes, and I knew he would be missed. I was therefore having a bout of imposter syndrome, seriously doubting how I would be able to fill his shoes. At that moment, I felt it would have been easier to be replacing Major The Honourable Laurence John Evelyn Twisleton-Wykeham-Fiennes – at least my name was shorter!

Looking back, I shudder a little recalling how I approached my address to the squadron that morning. The issue was not what I said or the words I used. It was *who I was being* as I said them. My self-doubt pushed me towards trying to mirror what I saw in Ian – my experience of him as a person. At one level, there was some logic to it: after all, why not emulate someone who had been very successful when in my role? Why change anything?

Just be like him, said the voice in my head.

Of course, however I came across – how I *occurred* – to my people seated in front of me in the briefing room, it was nothing like Ian. The trouble was, how I occurred was nothing like the true me either. It was an act – an act that felt as uncomfortable to me as it likely did to those in the room. I'd fallen into the trap of feeling I needed to change in order to assert power and control in my new role. I had become a different version of myself. Just as a fake Rolex watch could never be like the real thing, I may have looked like the same Peter Docker, but there was something not quite right.

We can all instinctively sense when there is a disconnect between how a person is behaving and whether that is true to who they are. We might not always be able to put words to that feeling, but we will always know if it doesn't feel right. And when that happens, trust is the first thing to evaporate.

BACK TO CLARITY

In the weeks that followed, I could tell that people on my squadron were having difficulty working out how to relate to me. Some of them knew me from the past, before I had become the boss, and were probably subconsciously confused about the person they saw now and didn't recognize. The unsettled atmosphere made conversations awkward and made leading all the more challenging.

It took me about six months to relax into my job, shake the fear of failure, and build the humble confidence to be myself.

I started to bring my own humanity and character to the role rather than sheltering behind the image of who I thought I should be. This in turn enabled others to better connect with me, and trust started to recover.

The key to this shift was returning to my stands – those things I felt to be really important.

One stand in particular gave me the focus I needed: the potential of others and giving them the opportunity to grow into that potential. I began to spend the vast majority of my time spotting the abilities and talents of my people and helping them grow. Instead of being preoccupied about how I might be compared with my predecessor, I became absorbed in how I could help build and support those who might take my place in the future.

While I didn't always get it right, the story I shared in Chapter 1 suggests my overall trend was in the right direction: Simon, Phil, and Al all subsequently became squadron commanders. In addition there were Dan, Jamie, Kevin, and Steve – also junior officers on my squadron at the time – who all rose to command their own. Several of those men have since been promoted further, beyond the rank I held on retiring from the service.

Looking back, what I saw in each of them was the capacity and willingness to lift others up and not just focus on themselves. They showed the courage needed to take ownership of difficult situations, run towards challenges, and overcome setbacks. In other words, they each demonstrated aspects of what I now call Jumpseat Leadership.

Everything these officers have achieved has been done on their own merits, supported by the opportunities that came from the high number of operations we had at the time and the role of our squadron. But I believe I was able, as their commanding officer, to give them the space they needed. This only became possible when I embraced who I was as a human being and stopped trying to be someone else.

INTEGRITY OVER AUTHENTICITY

As a young chap approaching the end of officer training, I recall receiving some leadership advice. It was simple: *Be yourself.* At the time, I don't think I fully appreciated the importance of these words. It's a notion we all take different lengths of time to truly grasp. It starts with getting clear on who we are as a person, what we stand for, and learning to lead ourselves.

For all of us, this process begins in adolescence, and it continues as we engage with the world and experience life. Whenever we subsequently find ourselves in a team or leading others, from any work situation to being a parent or mentor, it's vital to bring that clarity to the fore. It helps others to better relate to us. It builds trust, and consequently, we accomplish more. The importance of being myself was certainly a principle I seemed to temporarily forget when I took over my squadron. Much earlier in my career, as a frontline pilot, I had been at ease with myself. When I then rose to become a squadron commander, I initially became distracted by the weight of expectation I felt – the fear of not wanting to screw up or let people down. The more eyes that are on you, the harder it can be to stay true to yourself.

When we are being ourselves, one could say we're being **authentic** – our words and actions match who we are, how we feel, and what we believe. This has to always be a good thing, right?

Not always.

As the remarkably insightful American author, Seth Godin, observes, being completely authentic is a right we should relinquish when we're about ten years old. Babies cry when they're hungry. Toddlers scream and shout when they don't get what they want. Both these reactions are completely authentic. In each case, the behaviour reflects how the young person feels. But as we mature and become aware of how our reactions can affect others, we need to apply a filter. That filter is **integrity**.

In this context, integrity is about us tempering what might otherwise be our authentic reaction, by considering first what we stand for and, importantly, what is in service of those around us. For example, we wouldn't expect a doctor to say how terrible they felt while delivering news of a terminal condition. It wouldn't be in service of their patients. Equally, as a force commander during the Iraq War, it would not have served my people for me to share the concerns I felt about the days that lay ahead. Those men and women were looking to me for guidance and direction, not hesitancy and doubt – either of which would have likely fuelled their own fears. In a home setting, if we're lying awake at night in the face of losing a job and not being able to pay our mortgage, most of us would choose not to share that anxiety with a six-year-old child.

As my friend, accomplished industry leader Marian Stefani, points out, we need to offer the people in our team consistency in how we behave. The same applies to us as parents if we want our kids to develop a sense of right and wrong. This consistency is best built on our stands, since they will provide a solid foundation that will serve us in normal times and in times of crisis. Practising consistency calls on us to have the filter of integrity in place, regardless of how we feel.

FEEDBACK WITH INTEGRITY

Integrity is vital when offering feedback too. In the workplace I often hear the concept of giving people the *brutal truth*. It's a phrase typically reserved for when a manager or coworker feels the need to have a difficult conversation with a team member about their performance or behaviour. Or they might proclaim afterwards they *gave it to them straight*. While giving the unfiltered truth might be authentic, it will lack integrity if it's more about the manager or coworker getting something off their chest rather than being truly in service of the other individual and the team.

Equally, I recognize as a parent the times when, in years gone by, I've been frustrated about one of my children's school reports or a choice they've made. I soon learned that if I immediately reacted with my authentic feelings, although at times tempting, it was unlikely to get the best results, no matter how much I rationalized afterwards. I needed to take a breath first and make sure what I said to them, while addressing the reality of the situation, would also keep hope and possibility alive. Tough love is fine, provided it is genuinely in service of those on the receiving end and not just an excuse to vent our feelings.

Being authentic is frequently a reaction. Leading with integrity is a response.

TO BE INVITED

How will we know as an individual, and particularly in a formal leadership role, when we've built a foundation based on integrity?

The relationships we have with people will become stronger. They will feel at ease in our presence rather than being intimidated by our rank or position. Fear diminishes and is replaced by a culture of openness and possibility.

Let's return for a moment to San Francisco and the story of Calum, the newly qualified captain. You'll recall Calum had *invited* me to sit on the jumpseat for take-off. Let's dwell on that for a moment, because the invitation was everything. Inviting me to sit on the jumpseat was an unusual request. After all, it would be easy to assume, like a teenager who's just gained their licence and is able to drive unsupervised, that Calum would have been glad to see the back of me. Following his sign-off into his new role as captain, he was finally able to get on with his job without someone looking over his shoulder. But Calum saw me not as competition or a threat. He saw me as part of his team.

We could interpret his invitation to me as a sign he lacked

confidence and wanted to have someone more experienced there to back up his decisions. Even though this was not the case with Calum, inviting his boss back onto the flight deck was a gutsy call. It could easily have been seen by the rest of the crew as undermining his own authority as captain.

However, I could tell Calum felt entirely comfortable inviting me onto the flight deck. Equally, I felt entirely comfortable accepting and becoming part of *his* team, which *he* was leading. This reflects the relationship we had, the commitment we shared, and our respect for one another. None of this happened in the moment. It was built on a foundation established long before we set foot on the aircraft that day.

As with all relationships, the most generative tend to be those developed over time. In particular, it's the cumulative one-to-one moments we share that count, which might last only a few minutes or even seconds. It could be a brief exchange over coffee, sharing a cab ride, or spending a work lunchtime together sitting on a park bench. The bond is further strengthened if we jointly overcome some adversity, such as rushing through a busy airport security line and only just managing to catch our flight.

At the time, these moments may seem inconsequential, but combined, they help shape the picture we have of the other person. We begin to learn what they stand for and how they interact with people and different situations. Some of what we pick up during these moments we'll actively think about and store away, while much of it will be absorbed by our subconscious. As our image of the other person grows, so too does our understanding of what's important to them and what they stand for. If what we see fits with our own stands, trust emerges.

Calum and I had built a foundation of trust, which enabled him to be a leader driven by humble confidence, and it enabled me to have the humble confidence to take a step back and follow.

BEING SIGNIFICANT

In the late summer of 1977, NASA's two deep-space probes, named Voyager 1 and 2, were launched from Cape Canaveral for the start of their journey to explore our solar system and beyond. Both crafts have now entered interstellar space, travelling at over 35,000 mph. Incredibly, the probes will take 40,000 years to come anywhere close to another object – a distant star. Even then, that star will still be some nine trillion miles away. It's mind-boggling.

The Voyagers were able to leave our solar system because of what were now the tiny specks called Earth, our neighbouring planets, and the sun. As insignificant in size as those celestial bodies had now become, it was the combined gravitational force of several of them that enabled the probes to gather enough speed to continue their journey. The Earth and the sun also helped the probes to navigate.

For me, the effect of our solar system's planets on the Voyager probes is akin to the effect we can have on people. As leaders and coworkers, it is tempting to focus only on headline events, such as the completion of large projects or achieving significant milestones. These are obviously important, because a key part of leadership and being on a team is to bring about something that would not otherwise happen. But as Jumpseat Leaders, where at every level we intentionally lift up others along the way so they may eventually take the lead, it's the small, seemingly insignificant moments that are more important. It's the one-to-one exchanges we have with people that can have the most lasting impact on how they find their way and accelerate towards their potential. Usually without our knowing, those moments will continue to affect what those people subsequently accomplish long after we've gone.

We can all recall those people from our past who have had a major influence on our lives, including parents, teachers, mentors, friends, or work colleagues. There is a high chance they will not realize the effect they've had on us. It's as if they had been a planet in the solar system, totally unaware of their influence on Voyager 1 and 2. To them, what they said or did would have been insignificant and quickly forgotten.

FLEETING MOMENTS

In my thirties, I worked for a few years in the Ministry of Defence, or MoD, in London. The MoD fulfils a role similar to that of the US Pentagon and Department of Defense, and while there I helped develop and implement government defence policy. For about eighteen months, I had the privilege of working closely with the then Brigadier Jim Dutton, a Royal Marines Commando. He would later become Lieutenant General Sir James Dutton KCB CBE, knighted by Her Majesty The Queen and appointed her representative as the governor of Gibraltar, although he still went by the name Jim. He was my boss and two ranks senior to me when we both served at the MoD, although it always felt like we were in a partnership.

By any measure, Jim was – and still is – a remarkable leader. A quick internet search will reveal his many accomplishments. But for me there was one fleeting moment that captured everything.

Jim had just stepped out of his office on his way to give an important briefing to the prime minister. I happened to be in the corridor at the same time, and he paused as he was about to pass me. Opening the folder of briefing documents clutched in his hand, he asked me my view on one of the key issues. Now, whatever the subject was I cannot remember, and who knows if he used my input. But that's not the point. It was the way he listened intently to my answer that will stay with me.

In that moment, he lifted me up. I felt heard, and when people feel heard, they tend to contribute more. Discretionary effort – the energy people choose to bring to their work – increases. The moment lasted less than 20 seconds, but it cemented my drive to go above and beyond for Jim as a leader. More than that, it inspired me to look for opportunities to practise the same approach whenever I was leading, both day-to-day with my colleagues and later in a more formal capacity.

While those fleeting yet significant moments can be created by those senior to us, they can also come from those we lead. Most poignant for me was a brief exchange with one of my aircraft maintenance engineers on our return from the Iraq War in 2003.

We had just landed back at our base in the UK, after several months away in the Saudi Arabian desert. Friends and relatives, desperate to grab a long-yearned-for hug with their loved ones, gave us a big welcome and crowded around our three aircraft as we deplaned. There was jostling with the press reporters, equally keen to capture our reactions and clinch an interview for the evening news.

Eventually, with reunions completed, the crowds started to disperse as we all made our way home. I loaded my bags into my car and was about to drive off, when there was a knock on my side window. I looked up and saw John, one of the engineers who had been deployed with me. On one arm he had his tearfully happy wife and, clasped tightly with the other, he held his newborn son, whom he had just met for the first time. I rolled down the window and asked what I could do for him. John looked at me with a big smile on his face and said, "Sir, I just want to say ... thanks for bringing us all home safe."

I find myself quite emotional as I write about this, just over eighteen years later. Back then, all I could manage was to return his smile and blurt a swift "You're welcome" before driving away. The picture of this family standing at my car window, the sacrifices they had made, and John's simple words, combined to really emphasize the greatest accomplishment of my time leading during that conflict: everyone came home. I doubt whether John remembers that moment or the words he said. I'll remember them for the rest of my life.

WHO AM I BEING?

I had completed a workshop session for a large group in Melbourne, Australia, and it was time to catch my flight to Sydney to prepare for my next event. Unfortunately, when I arrived at the airport, I was faced with a scene of chaos.

It was Friday night, and several thousand passengers were anxious to get home to Sydney. Many people commute between the two cities during the working week, and there are plenty of airlines more than happy to accommodate them. Only on this Friday, all the aircraft heading to Sydney had ground to a halt. A large belt of thunderstorms was sweeping across the east coast of the country, and all departures to the city had been held.

As the delays mounted, more and more flights started to get cancelled. Frustrated passengers clambered to switch to flights still showing as active, and tempers began to flare as heated exchanges took place with the gate agents and airline representatives. What made it worse was that the weather in Melbourne seemed fine, so the reason for the disruption was not immediately obvious.

It had been a long day, and I decided to just settle back and put my trust in the airline gods that my flight would eventually be called. Remarkably, after a delay of about three hours, I saw the information screen change to "Boarding now", and I soon found myself sitting on the front row of the Qantas Boeing 737, watching all the other passengers come aboard.

I didn't envy the senior flight attendant. The mood at the departure gate had been pretty ugly, and he was about to have an aircraft packed full of largely tetchy, tired, and impatient bodies, who were in no mood for any further hold-ups. I know from a pilot's perspective how frustrating and unpredictable weather delays can be, but generally I would be safely on the other side of a flight deck door. It's the cabin crew who have to deal with passengers' raw emotions.

What I wasn't expecting was the masterclass I was about to witness on how who we're being can completely shift a situation and the results that follow.

As each passenger stepped through the door, Matthew, the flight attendant, took their boarding pass and welcomed them by name. He apologized for the delay and explained why the weather at Sydney had slowed the flow of traffic. He went on to say how the captain was loading more fuel in case of any other delays during our flight because of the storms, and that he and his colleagues would do all they could to make their trip as swift and comfortable as possible.

This was not a script he was using. Matthew slightly modified what he said to each passenger, so it remained fresh for those waiting in line behind. As a family of four boarded, Matthew spotted it was the son's seventh birthday, so he knelt down to the lad's level, congratulated him, and promised him a treat from the snack trolley a little later.

Did Matthew need to do any of this? Not at all. Was he frustrated with the delays and just wanting to get home too? Probably. But approaching this situation with *integrity*, in his role as the senior flight attendant, was not only the right thing to do – it was the smart thing too. The way he was being, and how he occurred to each and every passenger, had two immediate effects.

First, the slight delay he caused at the door by chatting meant every passenger had time to get to their seat and stow their bag in a locker without disrupting fellow passengers. This prevented arguments. Second, by the time boarding was complete, the mood on the aircraft was entirely different from how it had been at the departure gate. People were smiling, being courteous and generally pleasant to one another. Matthew knew this was not only good for the passengers, it was good for him and his team of flight attendants too.

Our 90-minute flight to Sydney was extended for half an hour as air traffic control kept us in the holding pattern until the bad weather had cleared. I didn't hear a single complaint from my fellow flyers. The cabin crew had continued to keep the atmosphere pleasant and cordial by the service they provided. I managed to take Matthew to one side during the flight and congratulate him on how he had handled what could have been a plane full of difficult passengers.

"There's no such thing as a difficult passenger," Matthew replied. "It's how you respond that makes them difficult."

THINK SMALL

As Maya Angelou once reflected, "I've learned that people will forget what you said, people will forget what you did, but people will never forget how you made them feel."

Who we are being – how we occur to others – fundamentally affects the outcome of any situation. It plays a part at every level, not just when we reach a senior leadership position. When we are able to show up with integrity, and have those we lead feel we *care* for them, we show our humanity. It's usually the small – to us seemingly inconsequential – moments that create the human connection we need to lift others up and have them feel heard and seen. Like the effect of the sun and the planets on the Voyager probes, we may be totally unaware of the impact we have on the lives of others and how we affect their course in life.

Whenever we sense our team is not accomplishing all that they could, it's always worth asking ourselves as leaders, *Who am I being that is causing those around me to be who they are?*

—— CONSIDER THIS ——

Whatever we do is only half the equation. Who we're being is equally important.

◆ LEARNING TO FLY

Consider this: We do not live in isolation. If we are to thrive in life, then we need to interact with others.

Progress accelerates when we're clear on what we stand for and investing in that through what we do, *and* notice how we occur to others as we're doing it. Get the "being" right, and the doing will follow.

The next time you feel the weight of expectation on you, who will you choose to be? Will you choose to be yourself, or will you try to be what you think others are expecting? One builds trust; the other doesn't.

◆ **FLYING**

Consider this: If things aren't working out as you would like, ask yourself, *Who am I being that is causing those around me to be who they are?*

Be yourself. In other words, stay connected to what you stand for and seek consistency in how you occur to others.

The next time you're faced with a tough situation, choose to act with integrity. By staying consistent with your stands, the more trust you will build and the stronger your relationships will become.

◆ **TEACHING OTHERS TO FLY**

Consider this: We set the tone – the context – within which people will grow. If we show empathy, care, and concern for our team, they will see that as important and will more likely be that way with others too.

Make time for the seemingly insignificant one-to-one moments – these are the ones people will remember. When people feel empowered and lifted up by you, it will inspire their own leadership and encourage their greater contribution.

The next time your team gets together to blow off steam, whether that's at an offsite or at the local bar, take the time to show each of them they are being heard. Listen. Acknowledge their comments or feedback, and let them know how you are going to apply it. This will not only create an environment where feedback is celebrated; your whole team will want to contribute more.

◆ LEADING FROM THE JUMPSEAT

Consider this: People are remembered for how they affected others, not just what they did.

Nelson Mandela is known in South Africa as *the father of the nation* and continues to inspire to this day.

As a Jumpseat Leader, everything is less about what you do and becomes more about who you are being. Have your people really sense your support and backing as they lead and step into the unknown. It will make a difference now and far into the future.

The next time you share a moment with someone from your team, try to keep in mind that it may seem like an insignificant moment to you, but it could mean the world to them. How would you want them to remember that moment?

Chapter 9

Collective Genius

WHEN BEN RICH took over as boss of his research and development organization, he faced a daunting challenge. He had worked for the guy he was replacing, Kelly Johnson, since joining the team over two decades earlier, and Kelly would be a tough act to follow. His predecessor was loved and respected by all and, even on his day of retirement, was still as intellectually sharp as they came and way more knowledgeable about the industry than Ben was.

That was the least of Ben's problems, though. The organization itself was threatened. Their main customer was strapped for cash, orders had dried up, and their technology was being outpaced by the competition. Unless Ben could find new projects, they would likely be bought out and broken up. All this was compounded by their line of work being highly classified – so much so that very few people even knew they existed. Because of this, their client base was very limited, and he wouldn't be able to simply advertise their services to get the business they needed.

Less than five years later, Ben had turned the situation around and generated earnings that would give them a place in the Fortune 500 top companies list. So how did he do it?

Before I get into that, let's take a step back while I share a little more context.

SKUNK WORKS

Ben's organization is known as Skunk Works, the highly secretive development arm of the aerospace company Lockheed (now Lockheed Martin). Founded in 1943 and still operating today, Skunk Works has been responsible for the design and manufacture of some of the world's most cutting-edge military aircraft, including the U2, in which CIA pilot Gary Powers was famously shot down while flying over the Soviet Union in 1960. When Ben took over the department, it was January 1975. As the long Vietnam War entered its final months, the political and public appetite for anything military was at an all-time low. Interest for new projects, let alone funding, was exceptionally difficult to find. The outlook was grim.

Skunk Works' biggest competitor was America's main global adversary, the Soviet Union. The technological arms race between the two countries was constant. At the time, the Soviets had excelled in their development of air defence missile systems, leaving America and the West highly vulnerable should any conflict between the two superpowers arise. During the height of the Cold War, it was the balance of military capability that maintained a fragile peace, preventing tensions from heating up and boiling over into a conflict that would affect the entire globe. The Soviets were also exporting their technology to many countries around the world, and this was further increasing tensions. In simple terms, in a war American aircraft would get shot down by highly superior Soviet missiles.

A TIME FOR LEADERSHIP

As a leader, Ben clearly had an uphill challenge. But he was the guardian of hope, determined his organization would be able to secure their future. Ben also realized he was a very different character from his predecessor, Kelly, who at the time was also one of the world's leading aircraft designers. Kelly had led by knowing the answers to technical problems and directing his people. Although accomplished in his field, Ben didn't have that level of encyclopedic knowledge. He needed a different approach.

In his excellent book, *Skunk Works*, Ben recalls how, in the early days of his tenure, he gathered his department heads and told them he was not a genius like Kelly. He explained he would be decisive in telling them what he wanted, but then would stay out of their way so they could get on and do it. Ben also promised to keep politicians and military officers off their backs so they could focus on their work. This was Jumpseat Leadership in action.

Shortly afterwards, a young mathematician and radar specialist on the team, Denys Overholser, came forward with an idea. He had come up with a theory, drawn from an old, very obscure Russian technical paper on how objects reflect energy to show up on radar screens. He proposed a new aircraft design that would render a plane invisible to enemy radars. Denys's idea was so radical that many of the more senior Skunk Works specialists thought it was theoretical nonsense. The fact that the mathematics involved could barely be understood by anyone, including Ben, certainly didn't help his case. Ben, however, was convinced there was potential and chose to have faith in Denys and back his idea. He directed his team to tear up the rulebook of traditional design and figure out how to bring Denys's theory to life.

Innovation flourished.

The result was the highly successful F117A Nighthawk, which looked like some sort of alien craft. Despite some setbacks along the way, the production version of the Nighthawk did exactly what Denys had predicted: it was able to fly through any radar system completely undetected. The F117 had made all the advanced Soviet missile defences entirely redundant. In achieving this, Skunk Works had redressed the balance between the two superpowers, helping ensure the Cold War stayed cold. Fifty-nine operational aircraft were built, creating $6 billion in revenue and cementing the future of the Skunk Works team.

Ironically, as Ben Rich recalls in his book, Kelly referred to the Nighthawk project in its early days as "theoretical claptrap". It seems highly likely that if Kelly had still been in charge, the aircraft might never have seen the light of day.

LEADERSHIP TRANSITION

The challenge facing Ben Rich when he took over Skunk Works in 1975 is equally a challenge for many of us today: how to thrive when promoted into a leadership role where we can't be the expert in every aspect of the work, while also enabling those in our team to thrive.

This challenge will occur for one of two reasons. Either, as in Ben's case, the expertise of individual team members is so specialized that we do not have the time or ability to learn and understand every nuance. Or the breadth of our responsibility is so wide, it's practically impossible to retain up-to-date knowledge of every detail. Whichever is the case, it can be a daunting moment the first time we find ourselves in this position. It's also a critical moment, since how we choose to lead will either accelerate or severely hinder our team's progress. The problem is that many of us fail to recognize this transition and few of us are trained to handle it. When we move from our comfort zone of being an expert in our field (which is usually the reason for promotion) to being decidedly outside our comfort zone and no longer the expert, it's difficult to let go. It goes against our instincts, especially if the work is really important to us, such as when we're the founder of the organization or the outcome is critical.

What tends to happen is we continue trying to lead as a subject matter expert, or we end up micromanaging and getting in our people's way. Even Gene Kranz, who led through the Apollo 13 crisis, fell into this trap early on in his flight director career. As he explained in an interview for the Smithsonian National Air and Space Museum in 2019, the toughest thing he had to do was to learn to listen. Rather than jumping in and trying to make every decision, he had to relax into taking a step back and allowing his specialists to make their own decisions. He realized his job was to stay focused on keeping a clear picture of where they were heading, learning to ask the important questions rather than being preoccupied with knowing the answer, and trusting in his people's ability and training to figure it out.

I had my own experience of this transition in 2004, when I was promoted to the rank of group captain (equivalent to colonel in the army or captain in the navy). With that promotion came the role of senior military lead for a £13 billion equipment project. I worked alongside my super-astute and dependable civil service counterpart, Chris Dell, and we both reported to another civil service colleague, the ever-calm and unflappable Kevin Johns. The project was highly complex and on our team we had specialists in engineering, infrastructure, communications, IT, export licensing, contracts, law, flying training, operations, logistics, finance, and civil-military partnerships, to name a few.

There was simply no way I could acquire all the expertise required to understand and make each and every decision across all these fields. Even attempting that would have been a poor use of my time and would have slowed progress.

Instead, my role was to keep everyone focused on what we were aiming to do, listen to the members of my team, and try to ask the important questions. I also needed to become adept at taking stock of the issues and identifying what really mattered so I could brief senior government ministers and negotiate with international partners. Fortunately, my military career to that point, not least my time during the Iraq War, had given me some preparation for this, but it still came as a big step up.

WHAT IT TAKES

Navigating this transition effectively calls on us to lead with humble confidence, bringing us back to a key component of Jumpseat Leadership.

Using Ben Rich as an example, leading with humble confidence enabled his team's success. Without this in place, nothing that followed would have been possible. If instead he'd had ego at the helm, Ben's preoccupation with himself and his own fortunes would have got in the way. His leadership would have been driven by fear – fear of personal failure, fear of inadequacy, fear of not matching up to his predecessor. Instead, Ben's willingness to let go of ego was front and centre when he gave his talk to his department heads. Right from the start, he made it clear he was not like the old boss, Kelly, either in intellect or style. *Who Ben was being* when he said this was important: when letting go of ego, it does not mean we give in to self-doubt or timidity. Ego must be replaced with humble confidence.

To show this degree of vulnerability took immense courage, but by doing so, Ben set the foundation for the future relationship with his team. He opened up the possibility for the team's trust in him, as their new leader, to emerge.

Ben also retained focus on what really mattered: the survival of the organization and the role they had to play in the defence of the nation. He was clear on what he stood for – what he felt was important. He was prepared to take the big decisions that were his to take, guided by the information made available to him. He kept hope alive even through the inevitable setbacks. Most of all, he lifted others up, showing faith in the ability of his people, such as Denys Overholser. He held the space for them to innovate and to grow without constant interference from above, from him or from others.

EMPOWERING THE COLLECTIVE GENIUS

The approach taken by Ben Rich is an excellent example of how to transition from *being an expert* to *leading the experts*. It's also an excellent example of how to lead in situations when we don't know the answer, such as when we are facing the unknown, in a crisis, or trying to create a breakthrough when we're stuck. When we're first confronted by these types of situations, by definition no one knows the answer. But collectively, a well-led team can figure it out.

When we limit what our team can do by remaining within the bounds of what we ourselves as leaders know, it severely hinders what we can achieve. The leader becomes the drag holding back progress. This is also true when we're leading our own lives, ignoring the wisdom of others, and choosing instead to go it alone. However, when we release ourselves from the need to be the expert in everything and learn to be comfortable leading when we don't know the answer, not knowing becomes a strength in itself – we are no longer limited by our own knowledge. Instead, we focus on being able to tap into the expertise and experience of those around us, by asking the important questions and learning to listen. And when we can do that, our fear of the unknown diminishes. Quite the opposite – we begin to relish the opportunity of the next unsolved challenge because we're confident that, as a team, we can figure it out. By empowering those on our team, we also build our ability as a Jumpseat Leader.

Richard Branson, the British entrepreneur, takes this approach to the next level. As he says:

> It's all about finding and hiring people smarter than you. Getting them to join your business. And giving them good work. Then getting out of their way. And trusting them. You have to get out of the way so you can focus on the bigger vision.

WHEN WE THINK WE KNOW

Of course, there will be those times when we feel we already know the solution to a problem or how to do a particular task. When that happens, I keep in mind a story once told to me by Daryl, a distinguished and cordial gent I met through a mutual friend shortly after I'd left the RAF. Daryl's primary work was as a voice coach for A-list actors. For many years before that, he had travelled the world as a sought-after tuner for a concert grand piano manufacturer. Helping people and instruments find their voice was clearly his skill and passion.

After leaving school at fourteen, Daryl started his working life at a piano factory in London, tasked with sweeping the floors. On his first day he went into the workshop, surrounded by beautiful pianos in different states of production, and started sweeping. After only a few strokes of his brush, one of the piano craftsmen called out for him to stop, yelling, "You're doing it wrong!" Taken aback, Daryl paused, wondering how difficult sweeping a floor could be. The craftsman came over and offered to show him. First, he grabbed a bucket of sawdust and soaked it with water. He then sprinkled the wet sawdust across the workshop floor. "It stops the dust on the floor kicking up as you sweep and coming to rest on the pianos," he explained. In that moment, Daryl promised himself he would always seek to ask others how they did a job, even if he felt he already knew. Indeed, he attributes his subsequent professional success to this simple, humble maxim.

When we think we know the answer, giving someone else the opportunity to share their answer first gives them the chance to rise and grow. It also gives us the opportunity to learn. And it might help avoid kicking up the dust, creating unnecessary effort, and causing unintended consequences.

PROBLEMS AND CHALLENGES

It feels good to know the answer, to be the go-to person, whether that's at work, at home or in any other situation. This is natural, stemming from how our culture encourages us through our school years and early career to specialize and become proficient in what we do. So it's little wonder many of us gravitate towards becoming increasingly expert at solving problems in our chosen field. While this is absolutely valid, it can only take us so far. If we want to go further, we need to find the vulnerability to feel comfortable in *not* knowing the answer.

In the 1990s Ronald Heifetz of Harvard Business School identified the difference between what he called a **technical problem** and an **adaptive challenge**. In simple terms, a technical problem is one we've likely come across before, such as the printer running out of ink or being low on stock in our warehouse. We know what the problem is, it's clearly defined, and we also know the solution. We deal with technical problems by telling people what to do and how to do it. The solution to a technical problem is usually swift and easily found.

Adaptive challenges, on the other hand, are different. We don't know the answer, and no single individual on our team knows either. Sometimes, we might not even be sure what the challenge is, or worse, try to deny it exists because our ego drives us to stay in our comfort zone of knowing the answer.

When Gene Kranz was faced with the Apollo 13 crisis, no one knew what had caused the explosion, the damage it had done, or what the consequences would be. In the first few minutes after disaster struck, it would have been pointless for Gene, or anyone else, to start trying to come up with "the answer". It was the same for Ben Rich at Skunk Works. At first, he didn't know what would save the organization and secure their future. No one did.

Both Gene Kranz and Ben Rich solved their adaptive challenges by letting go of ego and leading with humble confidence. Rather than taking it upon themselves to know the answer, they created the psychological freedom needed for their respective teams to *learn* their way through to the solution. They gave permission for their people to take the lead – to take ownership and innovate, rather than waiting to be told what to do. Meanwhile, Kranz and Rich kept their focus on the outcome they wanted to accomplish, on the reason the outcome mattered, and on supporting their people.

WHEN THE STAKES ARE HIGH

Now, this approach may seem in some ways obvious, and yet it can be remarkably difficult to follow when the stakes are high. I know I have not always got this right in the past.

In recent years there have been two notable occasions, when I was facilitating workshops – one with David and another with Stephen, both close friends of mine and each highly talented. Each of the workshops was addressing an important adaptive challenge, and I felt pressure to ensure the sessions achieved the outcomes we were seeking. I became so focused on the results, and on carefully curating the workshops to get there, that I tightened my grip of control. On each occasion, I effectively shut David and Stephen out.

David told me afterwards he began to wonder why he was with me at the front of the room, since I wasn't giving him the space to contribute anything. Ultimately, he mentally withdrew and left me to it. At the time, I had no idea of this. I was blind. Although not a disaster, the session was not the success it would have been with the power of David's ability in play.

It was a similar experience for Stephen in the workshop we later cofacilitated. He felt a bit like a spare part. Fortunately,

I became aware of this before it was too late and let Stephen back in. And I'm so glad I did – the contribution he subsequently made was crucial to the success of the session.

Empowering others to figure things out can feel like relinquishing control at *precisely* the time we feel we should be tightening our grip. Fear creeps in. This is why, in practice, to lead a team through an adaptive challenge calls on everything we've discussed so far in this book. We need the clarity of what we stand for as an individual to give us the guidance and courage we need to take on the unknown. We need to foster a shared commitment that draws our team together in service of others and our cause. As the leader, we need to acknowledge the reality of the situation we face, while championing hope that together we will find our way through. Each of these elements positively affects how we occur to others, creating the environment in which our people feel able and willing to come forward with their ideas.

This is harnessing collective genius.

ADAPTIVE CHALLENGES NEED ADAPTIVE SOLUTIONS

A little over a decade ago, my father-in-law, Peter, was approaching the stage in life where it becomes unsafe to drive a car. Although he was mentally sharp, his eyesight, hearing, and reactions had deteriorated considerably. But, like many people of senior age, he fiercely held on to his independence, and being able to drive was a key part of that. However, as a family, we were becoming increasingly concerned he would have an accident and potentially hurt himself or someone else. The question was how we could stop him driving while not completely destroying his self-confidence and freedom.

This was an adaptive challenge. Treating it like a technical problem by, say, removing his car keys would have undermined him and likely caused a lot of upset for everyone concerned. It may also have led to his mental decline. What we did instead was to open up the challenge to a virtual team – the wider family, his doctor, and charities that could offer age-related support and advice. It became clear that we needed to somehow allow Peter to *choose* to stop driving. Better still, rather than this being seen by Peter as him *stopping* something, we wanted him to see giving up his car as the opportunity to *start* something new.

Over the weeks that followed, we chatted to Peter to learn more about what his car meant to him. It turned out he found driving to be increasingly hard work, and he really only drove to the shops to buy food. Over several conversations, we asked Peter how the situation might be improved or what life would be like if he didn't need to drive any more.

As we all shared our thoughts, Peter started to make connections and see new possibilities. He remembered a local taxi service, owned by a trusted friend of the family, which he had used occasionally over the years. A week later, Peter suggested it was time to sell his car and use the money to pay for the occasional taxi ride to chauffeur him wherever he wanted to go. As a bonus, he would get to have friendly chats with the driver. Importantly, this was Peter's choice. While no longer driving himself, he remained empowered, feeling supported by his family and continuing to lead an active life. And, even though we had provided the catalyst, it was he who had also identified an advantage to this change.

Adaptive challenges arise frequently when people's perceptions are involved. In business, this can be when we're trying to implement change or shift a culture. Attempting to solve an adaptive challenge with a technical fix will rarely, if ever, work. For example, hoping to transform safety on a construction site, or quality control in a factory, by writing more regulations will do nothing if those who work there choose not to follow them. We end up spending more time, energy, and money on forcing people to comply, with little sustainable impact. Safety or quality-control issues are adaptive challenges, which need an adaptive leadership response.

A BLEND

Some issues that slow us down are a *blend* of technical problems and adaptive challenges. Just knowing this distinction helps us to approach them in the appropriate way. It's like the challenges in writing this book: I knew which computer program to use to type the words onto the page – that solved the technical problem. But the adaptive challenges have been first how to find the creativity to write, then how to shape the ideas, while also figuring out how to maintain focus and momentum. When it comes to editing and publishing, it calls on a lot of humble confidence to open up and receive the feedback and advice of others! To get to the point where the book is on a shelf in a store calls on empowering many people to contribute their knowledge. Collectively, we learn our way through to the outcome we seek.

Many of us seem able to adapt well when we're thrown into one particular common leadership role – one that calls on humble confidence. Indeed, it's a role that can be one of the greatest adaptive challenges of all. That role is parenthood.

I recall the day our first child was born and we brought her home. As for every new parent, there was so much my wife and I didn't know about what to do and what the future would hold, it was scary. We quickly sorted many of the technical problems with easy solutions – a baby car seat, clothing, nappies, a baby monitor, and all the other miscellaneous stuff we felt we needed. What took much more time was learning how to properly care for our daughter – those were the adaptive challenges. And yet there was no doubting our absolute commitment, and this gave us the courage to admit we didn't know all the answers. It led us to empower those around us to help figure it all out. We asked the midwife, the doctor, health visitors, our friends, and family, and particularly our own parents. We learned to ask better questions and listen to the answers.

A LEADER'S ROLE

Building the muscle that allows us to feel comfortable leading when we don't know the answer is a highly valuable skill to develop. It doesn't happen overnight – it's about practice. We can gradually learn to focus more on holding the space for others to come together and solve the new challenges we face, rather than relying on us, as the leader, being the expert. It releases us from our own limitations. We might not always get it right, but as we build momentum, we'll attract a team around us who want to be a part of whatever it is we're working on.

Having people choose to follow us into the unknown happens when we're willing to let go of ego and embrace humble confidence. The courage to do this is maintained by our commitment and *love for* what we're trying to achieve, rather than the *fear of* failure. Whatever the setbacks, we hold on to hope and instil it in others. We learn to listen and to challenge assumptions by asking the important questions. Together, these practices begin to create an environment in which those around us want to contribute their expertise and insights, giving us access to the collective genius of our team.

As we lift our people up, just as Ben Rich did with Denys Overholser, the outcome can be as surprising as it is remarkable. The beauty is that we don't need to attend college or spend years studying technical subjects to achieve this way of leading. We all have access to this right now. It's within each of us. We simply need to choose to let it emerge, and that can start at whatever point we are at in our Jumpseat Leadership journey.

—— CONSIDER THIS ——

As leaders, we can mistakenly believe that we need to be the person to provide the answers to all the problems our team faces. This saps our energy and our capacity, and creates an environment in which our people wait to be told what to do. A Jumpseat Leader focuses instead on building their ability to lead when they don't know the answer, creating the environment where they can harness the collective genius of their team.

◆ LEARNING TO FLY

Consider this: Practise the power of "not knowing", by asking questions at every opportunity, with a keen interest in listening to the answers.

It's empowering to be able to say, "I don't know – please explain", or "Show me", even when you think you do know the answer, because you will still nearly always learn something new. When *learning to fly*, there is no expectation for you to know, so take full advantage of it! This is an exercise in humble confidence.

The next time you are asked to do something you have never done before, pause and ask, "Before I begin, is there anything you wish you had known before you did this?" Really listen. Even if you don't learn anything new, it is a great way to build relationships. Who doesn't want to be around someone who is willing to learn and is open to advice?

◆ FLYING

Consider this: It's said that the pilot with 500 hours' flying time in their logbook is at their most vulnerable. In other words, they have enough experience to think they know what they're doing and therefore stop taking the opportunity to learn.

Remind yourself that you do not know all the answers, and beware of complacency. The next time you finish doing something, pause before turning it in or hitting the send button. Go through a quick mental checklist or, better yet, jot down all the steps you needed to take to sign it off as complete. If you work with a team, this is a great exercise to do together.

◆ TEACHING OTHERS TO FLY

Consider this: Focus on holding the space for others to contribute to the answers, while remaining connected to the shared commitment. This is particularly important when leading a team of experts from different fields.

Language is important – ask "What's missing?" instead of "What's wrong?" Acknowledge all contributions, even if they don't seem to be what's needed right now – these could be useful stepping stones to the answer. Create a culture where people feel encouraged to voice their ideas even if they are not sure about them.

The next time you are leading a meeting, instead of *telling* your team what to do, *ask* them to walk you through what *they* feel the next steps should be. Ask if any updates or changes need to be made. Seek their recommendations and share best practices so everyone can learn – including you.

◆ LEADING FROM THE JUMPSEAT

Consider this: You should be reaching the point where you are no longer making most of the decisions. However, you can still foster a culture of learning and listening.

Continue to be curious. Pay attention to who you are being when you're asking questions, so you're not perceived as a backseat driver. Support and endorse the decisions made by others when you can. If you feel you can't, wait until the end of the conversation before you jump in. Seek to understand the solutions they want to bring to the table.

Ask yourself what was missing from when you were *teaching others to fly*, or what you could have done to support them flying on their own.

When you walk into a meeting room or enter a video call, take note of what happens. Do people stop talking and look to you for solutions? Do you immediately offer solutions rather than asking the team for their input? Write down every time you supported rather than stepped in. Do you give your team the opportunity to learn, or do you take over?

Sometimes you may be the only one who has the solution, and that is okay. But before you offer your thoughts, wait until everyone has spoken.

— BELONGING —

—— Chapter 10 ——

Finding the Connection

IN JANUARY 2020 my work took me to Amman, Jordan. What I learned while touring the city deepened the connections I had to the area in ways I had not anticipated. The trip completely shifted my perception of what's possible and led to one of the most fascinating conversations of my life.

While I had visited many Arab nations before, this was my first visit to Jordan. This beautiful country has its longest border with Saudi Arabia, which lies to the south and east; with Iraq, Syria, and the disputed region of Palestine and Israel as its other neighbours. My host, Wajeeha Al Husseini, generously gave up her time to show me around their hilly capital, Amman. We drove and walked around the city, which buzzed with life and energy as people went about their business. Some of the scenes, such as the colourful and aromatic spice markets, or souks, and the dazzling gold quarter with its lavish rings, necklaces, and bracelets, were familiar to me from other Arab countries I'd visited. Others were unexpected and breath-taking, including the ancient Jabal al-Qal'a, or Citadel Hill, with its Temple of Hercules; and the Roman amphitheatre, built in the second century, which can seat 6,000 people and is still in use today.

What struck me most was the atmosphere, the culture – the way the city felt. There was a wonderful mixture of East meets West, of civility, and of a sense of live and let live, mutual respect, and harmony. This stood out because it's not necessarily the same in the countries that surround Jordan. I was quietly reflecting on this as we walked back towards the car, when Wajeeha pointed out a school that had an excellent reputation. "It's run by Catholic nuns," she explained. "It's really good, and quite a few Muslim families send their kids there too."

This took me by surprise. Jordan is predominantly a Muslim country, and I had assumed – probably reinforced by what I read and see in the Western news – that there would be discord or, at best, tolerance between the major religions. I didn't expect to see such integration and acceptance. Sensing how my preconceptions had been turned on their head, Wajeeha smiled gently and said, "Let me tell you about my family in Jerusalem."

THE HOLDER OF THE KEYS

Across the Jordanian border, to the west, is Jerusalem – a unique place that is holy for the Islamic, Jewish, and Christian faiths. The Church of the Holy Sepulchre sits in the northeast part of the city and is recognized by many to be built on the site where Jesus was crucified and buried. The church itself has had quite a turbulent history, having been built originally in the early fourth century, burned down in 614, and rebuilt over the following two decades. It was destroyed once more in 1009, restored again, and then completely rebuilt in the twelfth century.

The current church was constructed in the 1800s. Its past perhaps reflects the volatile nature of this part of the world. But amid the turmoil, one tradition has held strong for more than 800 years: members of Wajeeha's family, who are Muslims, have kept the only keys to the door of this church. Even today they *continue* to hold the keys, by invitation of those who worship there.

In our modern world, in which there seems to be so much division that is often based around religion, this symbol of cooperation and trust seemed remarkable to me. I wanted to learn more. A few months later, thanks to Wajeeha, I was able to speak directly with Adeeb Jawad Joudeh Al Husseini, the current holder of the church keys, and his brother, Sari Joudeh.

Sari explained to me how, in 1187, the Muslim sultan, Saladin, led a successful military campaign to take back Jerusalem from Christian crusaders, who had held the city for almost 90 years. After his victory, Saladin committed to protecting all Christian holy sites, including the Church of the Holy Sepulchre, from being destroyed or converted into mosques. He was determined to create peace and tranquillity in the city for all Christians and to ensure this continued under any future Muslim rulers who might succeed him.

Saladin consulted his people and the patriarchs – the most senior bishops representing the Christian denominations. Together they agreed the keys to the Church of the Holy Sepulchre would be held by a highly respected and influential Muslim family, whose history could be traced back to Muhammad, the founder of Islam. That family was Al Husseini. Since then, the keys have been passed down through the generations to Adeeb who, like his forefathers, ensures the church is opened each morning and secured every evening.

The role of the holder of the keys has been reinforced by multiple royal decrees from leaders over the centuries. But the bond between the Al Husseini family and the Christian community goes way beyond peaceful coexistence. Both Adeeb and Sari attended a Catholic high school, and their children now go there too. When Adeeb and Sari's father died in 1991, the Christian patriarchs came to pray over their father's body, in a moving act of respect and unity. Sari told me the next generation of his family is even more passionate about keeping the tradition alive, and with it the bond that brings the two religions together.

What Saladin put in place over 800 years ago, to end the cycle of destruction, was an act of courageous leadership, which chose a context of love over a context of fear. His legacy continues to bring people together and create a sense of belonging.

CONTEXT GIVES MEANING

Everything in our world can be seen as either **content** or **context**. Content includes what we say, the work we do, and the objects that surround us. Context, on the other hand, is what gives that content meaning.

Using the idea of a jigsaw puzzle again, the puzzle pieces are the content, while the context is given by the picture on the box. Without that picture, the puzzle pieces lack meaning – they're just oddly shaped pieces of cardboard with random colouring. Once we see that picture, they begin to make sense, and we can start to bring them together in a coherent way.

Before talking to Adeeb and Sari, it was as if I had a number of puzzle pieces – the keys, the church, and the relationship between Muslims and Christians – all floating around in my head without making any sense. Given what I knew, I was unable to understand how a family from one religion could hold the keys to one of the most sacred sites for another religion. Adeeb and Sari showed me the picture on the box – they gave me the context I needed. Suddenly, all the puzzle pieces came together. The more I heard from them, the clearer that picture became as I deepened my appreciation and understanding.

BUILDING RELATIONSHIP

The story of the holder of the keys is an enduring example of the possibility unlocked when we build our relationship with context. It can draw seemingly disconnected people and ideas together in a powerful way. When seen within the right context, we can uncover deep meaning that can help us overcome challenges and apparently insurmountable issues. In business too, a strong relationship to context can lead to extraordinary performance.

Deep in the Oxfordshire countryside in England is a luxury hotel and restaurant called Belmond Le Manoir aux Quat'Saisons. Founded in 1984 by French chef Raymond Blanc, the restaurant earned two Michelin stars on opening and has retained them every year since.

For over 90 years, Michelin has awarded restaurants one to three stars, judged on the quality of the ingredients used, cooking techniques, the personality of the chef in their cuisine, value for money, and consistency. Assessments are made anonymously by specially trained inspectors, who will visit a restaurant at least every eighteen months before making their award. One star equates to *very good*, and two stars is *excellent*, while three stars denotes *exceptional cuisine* when compared with other restaurants in the same price bracket. Michelin stars are much more rigorous and standardized than those awarded by reviewers on crowd-sourced apps such as Yelp. To put this in perspective, of the estimated fifteen million restaurants in the world, there are currently fewer than 400 that hold two Michelin stars. In the world of cooking, to have a double Michelin star is a remarkable feat, let alone keeping the award continuously for decades, as Raymond has done. What makes the achievement even more surprising is that Raymond has never had any formal training as a chef.

A few years ago, my work gave me the opportunity to meet and chat with Raymond on several occasions. I was immediately struck by the passion and respect he has for food, how it's grown and prepared, and his energy for sharing with others the way he sees the world. The grounds of the hotel are beautifully maintained, and Raymond explained how he encourages each of his trainee chefs to adopt part of the fruit and vegetable garden. He wants them to build relationships with the produce, the richness of the soil, the climate, and everything that enables the plants to grow well – collectively known as the *terroir*, as Raymond frequently refers to it. Before preparing lunch or dinner, the chefs will pick many of the ingredients directly from the gardens themselves, building a greater appreciation of nature's cycles and how to work with them. It seemed to me that Raymond is committed to nurturing the context where all of his chefs truly care for the food and dishes they create. He revels in the delight great cooking can bring and wants to share that feeling with everyone.

This sense of relationship and care extends into Raymond's kitchens. Even at the height of dinner service, there is very little noise or talking in the kitchen. There's no need. From the head chef to the waiters, washers, and cleaners, everyone knows their part, what's needed when, and how to integrate with those around them. Without the deep relationship every-one has with the food they're preparing, and with one another, and knowing how they fit in, none of the extraordinary dishes they create and serve would be possible. Raymond has painted a very clear picture on the puzzle box – a context – for all his people to see, and he invites them to become a part of it. At every meal service the pieces come together perfectly, time and time again. There is a palpable sense of belonging among everyone on the team, just like there is for every ingredient that finds its way into the remarkable menus they curate.

Although Raymond remains as chef patron, most of the cooking is done by those he has trained. He entrusts them with main-taining the standards required to keep those Michelin stars. He has become a Jumpseat Leader, lifting up others who share his passion for food and the joy it can bring. If proof were needed, 34 of the chefs he has trained over the years now run their own restaurants with their own Michelin stars.

CREATE THE CONTEXT

Although the circumstances were worlds apart, what the Sultan Saladin and Raymond Blanc each created was a context in which people could find meaning. That context enabled all those involved to build a strong relationship with what was important to them, while also defining new relationships with each other. Together, they generated a sense of belonging for everyone who chose to belong, leading to outcomes that were as extraordinary as they were unlikely.

When we create a context in which people feel they belong, and give them the support they need to do their job, it builds momentum. This in turn keeps the context alive for future generations, as it has for the son of Adeeb, who will take over the keys; or for the now celebrated chefs Raymond trained.

Context is vital for any of us to make sense of our world. As a leader, we may need to create that context so our team can find a way to relate and belong. At other times, it could be we simply need to adjust or *shift the context*.

SHIFT THE CONTEXT

When we **shift the context**, it's like turning over our jigsaw puzzle pieces and seeing a different picture on the other side.

The puzzle pieces haven't changed, but they take on a whole new meaning and can create a whole new picture, leading to different opportunities. This is what the London Taxi Company, the manufacturer of the iconic London black cab, discovered in a way that would transform its fortunes.

The history of the London black cab goes back several centuries. In 1621 the village of Hackney in Middlesex, England, started supplying London with horses to pull what became known as the hackney carriage. These days, horse-drawn carriages are long gone from the streets of London, and most of us will instead recognize the twentieth-century replacement, the black cab. Its design is as much a part of London's image as the yellow cab is for New York or the red urban taxi for Hong Kong.

The London Taxi Company can trace its roots all the way back to 1908, when it followed the UK government regulations to produce the first motorized black cabs that would replace horses, through to the more recent models that make up the 21,000 cabs on London's roads today. But in the last decade, the company has struggled to keep up with ever more demanding car engine-emission limits also set by the government. To survive, the business would need to take action and get ahead of the restrictions rather than constantly playing catch-up. A shift in context would achieve that – a shift that could potentially be as profound as the move from horses to motors over a century earlier.

In 2017 the London Taxi Company became the London Electric Vehicle Company, the new name signalling the shift in context. Their focus became the production of the first

155

purpose-built hybrid-electric cabs. To date they have built and sold over 2,500 of the new cabs and are rapidly expanding into fresh markets around the world. These latest vehicles continue to meet the principles set in 1908 and, importantly, honour the design legacy of the iconic black cabs that have gone before. Further innovation has followed, with the company now developing a completely new electric delivery van for city use, derived from the highly manoeuvrable and spacious cab.

The London Electric Vehicle Company has successfully turned over their puzzle pieces and is bringing them together with renewed vigour. The company still provides the means for hackney carriages to offer their services, only now it's within the context of embracing electric power rather than relying on diesel or petrol. There remains a strong sense of identity, history, and belonging, as their vehicles carry forward more than a century of tradition. The stringent car-emission legislation did indeed threaten the core of the company's near-term business. But viewed in the context of the long term, of opportunity rather than scarcity, it was an essential stepping stone, which led to the innovation that is now starting to secure their future.

WHEN CONTEXT FAILS US

While context gives meaning to what we do, becoming fixated on one particular context can limit us, since we can become blind to new opportunities. In the worst case, an unwillingness to shift the context can be disastrous.

A critical moment in the Apollo 13 story, which completely transformed the chances of the three astronauts surviving, was Gene Kranz's declaration that the mission was no longer about landing on the moon. It became solely about getting the astronauts back home safely. He shifted the context. This released fresh thinking around how the spacecraft and its systems could be used in ways never intended or even imagined by their designers, and proved to be key to solving the many challenges they faced. The resources the astronauts had out in space did not change, and yet the shift in context meant everything took on a different meaning.

While Apollo 13 was NASA's finest hour, what occurred on 28th January 1986 was at the opposite end of the scale. Seventy-three seconds after the space shuttle Challenger launched from Cape Canaveral, it exploded and was completely destroyed. Seven crew members were lost, including Sharon Christa McAuliffe, who was a teacher and the first civilian to fly a mission.

As the 2020 Netflix documentary series brought dramatically to life, the explosion was caused by a failure of the O-rings on the solid rocket boosters that propelled the shuttle during its first two minutes of flight. Like very thin rubber tyres with a circumference of almost 38 feet, these O-rings were fitted in pairs for redundancy, sealing joints between the cylindrical sections that made up each solid rocket booster. When a pair of these seals failed on Challenger, it allowed the burning gases inside to escape, ultimately leading to complete structural failure of the spacecraft. On the morning of the Challenger launch, the air temperature had dropped below freezing, causing the rubber seals to become much less flexible and even more prone to failure.

What's surprising is that the partial failure of these O-rings had occurred previously. Following each launch, the boosters were recovered for reuse, and damage was found after four previous shuttle launches. It was well documented by Morton Thiokol Incorporated (MTI), the manufacturers of the solid rocket boosters, who had made NASA fully aware. One of the design engineers, Bob Ebeling, had even stated that the shuttle would eventually explode if the O-ring problem was not fixed. So how was this situation allowed to continue?

Lawrence Mulloy, the NASA project manager in charge of the solid rocket boosters, knew about the O-ring problem. But he was driven by the shuttle programme being well behind schedule and by the need to catch up. Nothing else mattered. At the time Challenger was poised for lift-off, NASA had launched far fewer missions than they had promised to Congress. Mulloy knew it would take at least two years to redesign the seal and, to him, the further delay was not acceptable. He decided it was *not* risky enough *not* to fly, and gave a waiver for the shuttle launches to continue.

Mulloy's commitment was to the schedule and his reputation, not to flight safety and the lives of those on board. This was a context shared by his boss and likely reflected the *We can do anything* culture of NASA at the time. They were driven by the fear of losing funding, and the damage this would cause to NASA jobs and their reputation of getting things done, rather than being driven by love for the safety of their colleagues strapped into Challenger's seats. When later asked about the decision to launch, Mulloy responded, "If you don't keep to schedule, you don't keep your budget, so I put pressure on myself, just as a matter of pride."

Whether or not we agree with the single-minded commitment of Mulloy to keep the shuttle project going, the consequence of his pride and lack of humble confidence was disastrous. If he hadn't allowed ego to get in the way, he may have been more open to a shift in context towards safety when the risks started to compound. Rather than being rational and objective and delaying the launch, he became dogmatic, rationalizing the choices he made to have them fit into the context he wanted. Even on the morning of the launch, with clear statements from MTI that the cold temperatures increased the risk of failure of the O-rings, Mulloy insisted they pressed ahead, intimidating others until they withdrew their objections and conceded. His *stand for* the schedule turned into a *position against* those who got in his way.

After the disaster, context shifted back to flight safety, and the solid rocket boosters were redesigned. What followed were 85 successful launches over fifteen years, with no further problems. The irony is this could have been achieved by *choosing* to shift the context before the loss of seven lives. Tragically, this run of success was broken when the context shifted again away from safety. On 1st February 2003, the space shuttle Columbia broke up on re-entry, when some of its heat shield tiles failed. The investigation that followed revealed that this too was a known problem, which NASA had chosen not to address.

As Jumpseat Leaders, whatever context we choose, it needs to be built on the solid foundation of a commitment driven by love, not fear. This will help fuel the humble confidence we need to keep ego in its place, and for us to be willing to shift the context when it no longer truly serves others.

ILLUMINATE THE CONTEXT

Sometimes the context doesn't need to be created or shifted. The existing context simply needs to be **illuminated** – or reinvigorated – for each and every person involved, regardless of their role. As a leader, a focus on illuminating the context for all those on our team is an opportunity to help them feel they belong – to be seen and heard. And when people sense this, they bring their own energy and commitment to what the team is trying to achieve.

Four Seasons Hotels and Resorts sits at the top end of the luxury hospitality market. As a large business that spans much of the world, it seems more adept than most at illuminating the context for all who work there and for its loyal guests too. Established in 1960 by the Canadian Isadore Sharp, the company maintains a context focused on genuinely caring for people and creating extraordinary experiences. What makes this context so remarkable is that it's *applied to their employees first.*

This was all brought vividly to life for me in 2019, during the conference that Four Seasons held for their food and beverage team from across Europe, the Middle East, and Africa. I'd been asked to give a keynote talk and was invited to stay overnight.

The arrangements for the conference were made by the ever-calm and capable Mali (who at the time of writing manages the latest Four Seasons hotel, in New Orleans), and the setting she had selected – their hotel in Florence, Italy – was stunning. A renaissance palazzo–style property, with a walled garden and beautiful grounds, its rooms range from the equivalent of around $800 per night for the most affordable, to over $18,000 for the royal suite. For the duration of the conference, over 90 percent of the rooms were used to accommodate all their own employees who were attending the event. Luckily for me, as the keynote speaker, I was able to stay there too.

In the evening, in the hotel's fresco-filled lobby, Mali had arranged the most dazzling dinner and entertainment I have ever witnessed. This included sumptuous food and drink from local suppliers, a dance troupe, fortune tellers, and a poet who used a vintage typewriter to write personalized lines of verse for guests. The atmosphere buzzed with excitement, surprise, and delight. It's an occasion I will never forget, and I have the poem written for me framed and hanging on my wall at home.

This extravagant conference would have had a significant business impact, with rooms that weren't being let to paying guests and food costs much higher than a simple meal at a local budget restaurant. But this event reflected who Four Seasons are. There was no sign of slightly stale, cold sandwiches on paper plates, typical of so many company offsites, with employees milling around quietly plotting how to break away as soon as they can. Instead, Four Seasons took the opportunity to *illuminate* their context of caring and creating extraordinary experiences, showing exactly what this meant by offering it to their own people.

161

The event made the context real in a way that everyone could relate to and make personal. Like me, they would be able to recall that occasion, how special and valued it made them feel, and it would live on as a fond memory. Unless we have experienced a feeling ourselves, it's very difficult to work towards creating opportunities for others to feel that too. The first-class event acted as a reference point for how the company wants to make their paying guests feel. This doesn't mean the hotel would throw this type of party for every guest. Rather, the evening helped to inspire the ongoing company conversation of *How can we create extraordinary and memorable moments for our guests so they feel truly cared for?*

Showing they care is where Four Seasons really excels, for their employees and their customers alike. When we create shared moments that make us feel connected, we show that we care, and this nurtures a sense of belonging.

BEYOND EMPATHY

I often hear that empathy – the ability to understand and share the feelings of another – is a key ingredient of successful leadership. But in my mind, particularly for Jumpseat Leadership, empathy does not go far enough. If we are to create a connection with people – a sense of belonging – we need to go beyond the notion of empathy. We need to **genuinely care**.

Caring can show up in different forms. The drill sergeant who shouted and screamed at me for months during my initial training as an RAF officer seemed hard-hearted at the time. But his actions were sourced from genuine care, to help us build resilience under pressure and to draw us together. He knew these qualities, amongst others, would be needed during our years of service that would follow.

Equally, a great doctor will truly care for her patients. This doesn't mean she becomes absorbed in their pain and suffering, rather that she cares enough to see the human being and the fallout, not just the illness. An example could be taking the time needed to carefully talk a patient through their diagnosis at a pace that's right for them, rather than just bluntly delivering the facts.

Caring can be treating your people as you ask them to treat your customers, as so well demonstrated by Mali through the Four Seasons conference. It's perhaps no surprise the hotel group has the lowest staff turnover rate of any company in the industry and has consistently appeared in *Fortune* magazine's "100 Best Companies to Work For" every year since the survey began in 1998.

Caring can be as simple as finding the time to pause and listen to a member of your team, or to notice when something doesn't seem quite right in their world, and asking them how you might help.

Caring extends to our job too. We will only excel if we have a strong connection to our work and the context in which we do it. Raymond Blanc continues to be awarded two Michelin stars and has been able to train so many other Michelin-starred chefs because he genuinely cares for the food he prepares, as well as for the person who will eat it.

Empathy does not go far enough to nurture the sense of belonging that's needed for Jumpseat Leadership. As with every leader mentioned in the chapter, we need to show we care. And to care is to invest the only finite resource we have: our time.

CLOSER TO HOME

When we have a context that gives meaning to what we do, we can make it personal. And when we develop strong personal connection, we want to contribute, to help maintain what we've come to value. More than that, we want to share the experience with others so they may have the opportunity to make a connection too.

As a Jumpseat Leader, we have a role to *create*, *shift*, or *illuminate* the context of what we're working on, so those around us can make it relevant to themselves and *choose* to engage rather than being directed. One of the most powerful ways of doing this is to ensure that we, as the leader, maintain a strong personal connection to the context, so we continue to feel *we* belong. When we achieve this, it becomes obvious to those around us, and the connection becomes infectious. And it's equally obvious when we lose that connection.

There is no doubt about Saladin's absolute belief in the context he created in Jerusalem all those years ago. Otherwise, it would not have been passed down through the generations to this day. Equally, anyone who meets Raymond Blanc, or simply sees him on one of his television shows, is left with no doubt about his passion and the context he upholds for the power of cooking and food to bring joy. This context is taken forward by all chefs he has trained and most likely by the majority of those who have eaten in his restaurants.

Take a moment to reflect on the connection you have to the context of your work, family, and life. As a leader of others, or just when leading yourself, is the connection you have with the context, which gives meaning to all the content – the stuff – you're dealing with, as strong as it could be? If the answer is no, or if you're not sure, it might be time to create, shift, or better illuminate that context.

The stronger our connection, the more we will accomplish, and the more those around us will want to be a part of what we're building.

—— CONSIDER THIS ——

Whether leading ourselves or leading others, finding the connection that gives meaning to what we do is the key to accomplishing more.

◆ LEARNING TO FLY

Consider this: If you are struggling to make sense of something you are having to endure or feel to be arduous, adapt your relationship to it by shifting the context. *Shift the context, change the meaning.*

The next time you've been selected to present in front of your team, what steps can you take to strengthen and demonstrate your relationship with the context you've been given? Who can be a sounding board for you?

Ask someone you trust to help with any blind spots you may have.

◆ FLYING

Consider this: As you take on more and work with others, invest time in building as much relationship as you can with the tasks, the team, the context, and why all this matters to you.

The next time you're presented with a challenge, rather than trying to drive a square peg into a round hole, take a second to see if a shift in context is necessary. This could both reduce frustration and open up possibilities, by seeing the challenge in a different light.

◆ TEACHING OTHERS TO FLY

Consider this: Continue to build connection with the picture on the box.

When people become fixated on the puzzle pieces, give them the opportunity to stand back and rebuild the relationship to the bigger picture. The more you do this, the greater the sense of belonging – which leads to more innovation, loyalty, and discretionary effort.

Help others by illuminating the context for them so the work they are doing takes on more meaning. The next time team reviews come around, consider how you might help each person see you truly care for them as a human being. This will help build a culture in which they feel encouraged to care for their colleagues too.

Showing you care could be as simple as a listening session for you to better understand what inspires them away from work. These conversations strengthen connection, build understanding and camaraderie, and enhance a sense of belonging.

◆ **LEADING FROM THE JUMPSEAT**

Consider this: Since you are now taking a step back so others can step up more, seek opportunities to support by keeping the context alive.

The next time one of your products or services seems to have gone a little stale, bring your team together and ask them to illuminate the context. Perhaps the context has shifted a bit, and this illumination will allow everyone to get back on the same page.

——— Chapter 11 ———

Seconds Count

NOT EVEN TWO months had passed after the incident over Nairobi, Kenya, when I had been faced with crash-landing the aircraft after the wheels failed to lower. It was now 9th April 1988, and we were in the middle of our task to fly Sir Geoffrey Howe to official meetings scheduled in Bahrain, Kuala Lumpur, Singapore, and Brunei. We'd then return him to Bahrain, from where another crew would fly him back to London. The next day we would fly a different aircraft east again on an unrelated task to Sri Lanka, Hong Kong, and down to Sydney and Darwin in Australia, then back to Hong Kong, before returning home. For anyone, let alone me at the age of 25, this was one heck of a busy and exciting trip.

At the time, Sir Geoffrey was secretary of state for foreign and Commonwealth affairs, known more simply as the foreign secretary, responsible for Britain's relationships with other countries. A member of the government, he reported directly to Prime Minister Margaret Thatcher. Also on board we had Sir Geoffrey's assistants and officials, together with around a dozen press reporters, each of whom paid handsomely for a seat and the privilege of being able to capture any news first-hand. We also carried extra cabin crew, who were trained to provide the highest standard of food and service, using a vast array of fine china crockery and crystal glassware, which took up every inch of storage space in the galleys. With a total of 40 people on board an aircraft designed to seat 140, it was a very comfortable place to be as a passenger.

My captain for the trip was a highly experienced pilot, by the name of Jimmy Jewell. Jimmy had spent many of his early years in the RAF, flying Lightning fighter jets during the Cold War. He had the most meticulous and precise approach to his work and planned for every possible eventuality, giving him the capacity to deal with the unexpected.

In 1986 Jimmy had been flying Prime Minister Thatcher from Oslo, Norway, back to the UK. Shortly after take-off, air traffic control advised him they'd received information suggesting there could be a bomb on board. Unflustered, Jimmy spoke with Thatcher, and together they quickly concluded there wasn't much they could do about it in the air, so they might as well look for any bomb after they had landed in London. So that's what they did. Nothing much fazed Jimmy (nor, it would seem, Thatcher). Thankfully, the information turned out to be a hoax – a bomb was never found.

DOORS TIME

Exacting standards were expected of all crews operating these official flights, and Jimmy Jewell was an exemplar of how it should be done. No matter how far we were flying, we would

169

arrange to arrive at our destination on time – and I mean to the second. This precision timing was known as *doors time* – the moment the main passenger door would open and the most important passenger, known as the principal, would be greeted by the host nation. If we had the prime minister or Her Majesty The Queen on board, there would also be a red carpet at the aircraft steps, with a guard of honour and band as part of the formal welcome.

Arriving for doors time was a particular challenge, since this was before satellite navigation. We used the best available alternative back then, known as an inertial navigation system (which used motion sensors and gyroscopes to measure distance and direction travelled), plus a stopwatch and paper charts. We also had a navigator and an air engineer on the flight deck, and we would all work together on adjusting our flying speed to account for the wind during the flight, the different runways we might be expected to land on, and every possible permutation of taxi routing from the runway to where the red carpet would be.

During our approach to land, the navigator would give a running commentary on how many minutes and seconds to doors time, and if we needed to adjust our speed accordingly. After landing, as we approached the red carpet, the navigator would give the final countdown. At five seconds to go, the pilot would gently apply the brakes for the last time; at three seconds the aircraft would stop with the front passenger door exactly aligned with the red carpet; and, as the clock went to zero and the navigator called "Doors!", we would shut down all engines and the door would be opened, ready for the principal passenger to disembark. The entire crew worked seamlessly together to make this happen.

To arrive absolutely on time was not just a matter of the crew's professional pride. For a high-level official or state visit, to arrive early could embarrass the host nation, while arriving late could be construed as a diplomatic insult. And yet we needed to do all of this exceptionally smoothly, like a swan gliding across a lake, with our very important passengers having no idea of how hard we were working to make it happen.

WE'RE LATE

After being delayed on the ground by air traffic control for over 20 minutes, we had eventually taken off from Singapore, with Sir Geoffrey on board. We were now running late. The flight to Brunei on the island of Borneo in the South China Sea takes less than two hours, which meant we didn't have much opportunity to make up time.

One technique that helped was to fly a faster than usual approach to the runway, keeping our speed up at around 345 mph when normally we would be at about 200 mph. This was something we routinely practised and, providing the pilot reduced back to normal landing speed for touchdown, it was perfectly safe. Even if we were a little faster than usual on landing, it was still acceptable, as long as there was a long runway.

At Brunei airport that day, the weather was forecast to be fine, and the runway was twice as long as we needed to safely bring the plane to a stop, so things were looking hopeful.

Jimmy had given me the job of flying the aircraft, and I had started our fast approach. It was our air engineer who first spotted the potential problem. Still a few miles out from the airport, he saw that there seemed to be work being done on the first half of the runway, making it unusable. A quick radio call to Brunei air traffic control confirmed this – a significant piece of information, which had not been passed to us before leaving Singapore. Now we were coming in at high speed, with barely enough runway to land and stop.

I managed to get the speed back to the maximum allowed for landing, but as I tried to touch down smoothly, I misjudged, and the wheels hit the ground heavily. Worse still, I then had to stamp hard on the brakes, as the far end of the runway was rapidly approaching. My heart sank as, above the noise of the engines, all I could hear through the flight-deck door was the sound of dozens of pieces of fine crockery and glassware bursting from their containers and smashing on the galley floor. Our graceful swan had turned into an ugly duckling.

Soaked in embarrassment, I taxied the aircraft to the red carpet. Sir Geoffrey, no doubt stepping over broken plates and wine glasses, made his way to the door and descended the steps to be greeted by our Bruneian hosts. To add insult to injury, we had still arrived late.

BALLOON OF CONFIDENCE

As Sir Geoffrey was driven away for his meetings, there was an awkward silence on the flight deck. My balloon of confidence had truly burst. I felt I'd tarnished our reputation. I wished the ground could open up and swallow me whole.

Logically, given our delayed departure from Singapore, I knew there wasn't any more we could have done to have arrived on time. I also knew my touchdown had lacked finesse, to say the least, and the hard braking had been necessary to stop before we ran out of runway. But it had been me with my hands on the controls, and I took full responsibility. In my mind, I had let down Jimmy and the rest of the crew. I also felt really bad for the cabin crew, who had no doubt thought they had adequately secured the china and glassware; for our usual smooth arrivals, I'm sure their preparations would have been fine.

With the passengers now all off the plane, Jimmy glared at me across the flight deck as he climbed out of his seat. "I'm going to check on the cabin crew and the damage. You wait there."

I sat in silence and could hear Jimmy talking with the flight attendants down the back of the aircraft for a few minutes, before his footsteps became louder as he returned to the flight deck. Closing the door behind him, I braced for impact.

"What the hell was that?" he demanded. Before I could answer, he laid into me, barely able to contain his anger. "I thought you knew how to fly! That was embarrassing for the whole crew – it's a mess down there with broken crockery and glass all over the place. What Sir Geoffrey thought I can only imagine at the moment, but I'll find out when he returns for our flight tomorrow. I'll also make darn sure he knows it won't be you on the controls again."

For the next ten minutes I was on the receiving end of Jimmy's rant. He outlined the paperwork he'd have to fill in, the damage to our crew's reputation – not to mention to his own as captain – and the apology he'd need to make to Sir Geoffrey. With every second I felt smaller and more deflated. As Jimmy's voice continued to bellow, I started to think that perhaps I wasn't cut out to be a pilot on these official flights, after all, and should leave it to those who didn't make mistakes. At that moment, sitting on that flight deck, I wanted out. As my mind tuned back in to what Jimmy was saying, I realized he likely shared that view.

"For the rest of this entire trip, I will fly," he declared. "Since we don't have another pilot to replace you, until we return to the UK you'll remain part of this crew, but you'll be limited to the administrative tasks and talking on the radios to air traffic control. You won't get your hands on the controls again. That way there's perhaps a chance we can recover our reputation."

What was originally destined to be an exciting experience flying back to Bahrain, and then on to Australia and Hong Kong, turned into a chore. When we finally returned to the UK, Jimmy reported what had happened to our squadron commander, and I was removed from the cadre of pilots who flew the prime minister and other VIPs. From there my career seemed to spiral down further. I'd lost confidence in my own abilities, and I started to make other unforced errors. The chances of me becoming a captain started to fade into the far distance. The more time passed, the less I felt I belonged.

Only, that's not what actually happened. (And Jimmy, if you're reading this, forgive the poetic licence I've used to make my point.)

Let's rewind ...

As Sir Geoffrey was driven away for his meetings, there was an awkward silence on the flight deck. Not one known for smiling much, Jimmy seemed to glare at me for a moment across the cockpit. This swiftly evaporated, with his expression giving way to a mild grin as he quipped, "Well, at least everyone knows we've arrived!" That broke the ice, and everyone chuckled, including me.

I knew I wasn't off the hook yet. Jimmy would have been well within his rights to be annoyed with my handling of the aircraft. After all, while he had delegated the flying to me for that trip, he was the captain and the one who would have to respond to any negative feedback directed at the crew. It was his reputation on the line, and it would have been understandable if he had taken back the controls for the remainder of the trip, recommending I be removed from future high-profile flights. Jimmy could also have chosen to give me a detailed debrief on what I'd done wrong, labouring the finer points of aircraft handling.

Jimmy chose to do none of those things. He knew how I was feeling, since he'd likely made a similar mistake earlier in his career, and he could see through my quiet reflection that I took full responsibility. He didn't need to reprimand me or analyze my flying technique – I was already doing that myself.

What he needed to do was to draw me back in and have me feel I still *belonged*, as a valuable member of the team. He needed to help reinflate my balloon and restore humble confidence, so

175

I could show up without self-doubt getting in the way. Even so, what happened next took me by complete surprise.

Jimmy went on to explain how he and the navigator would go off to meet with air traffic control to talk more about the work on the runway and how it might affect our departure the following day. In the meantime, he wanted me to stay on board and, with the air engineer's support, start up the plane and taxi it to where it needed to be parked overnight, on the far side of the airport. We all knew this was not strictly allowed, since the entire flight deck crew should be present for taxiing. But the airport was quiet, with very few other aircraft around, and I figured Jimmy judged this act of trust in me would quickly restore the faith I had in my own ability too.

"And oh," said Jimmy as he got up to leave, "tomorrow I'd like you to fly the aircraft from here to Bahrain."

How Jimmy chose to lead in this situation was pivotal. It fundamentally affected how I went on to perform in the hours and days that followed. While I felt disappointed with my performance, I was able to quickly put it in perspective. This was largely because of the tone Jimmy set – one that enabled me to feel he had my back, that I still had a place on the team, and that I belonged.

We all sometimes fall below the bar we set ourselves. But it's how we recover that's important, and the leaders around us are those who have the power to accelerate that process. If Jimmy had chosen instead to allow his ego to be dented by how the events reflected on him, it's likely he would have taken it out on me in a way similar to the first version of this story. If he'd done that, it could have completely undermined the contribution I made on the next flight, with me becoming increasingly disengaged.

When someone on our team screws up, how we respond can have long-term consequences.

The next day, I flew well. In the months that followed, I went on to fly the prime minister and cabinet ministers another twelve times before starting my conversion to become an aircraft captain.

Looking back, in those critical moments on the flight deck in Brunei, Jimmy held the power to be the catalyst for positive growth in me *or* for potential decline, in equal measure. He chose to be a Jumpseat Leader.

The choices we make as leaders when faced with the mistakes of those on our team have consequences that extend well beyond the immediate situation. Seconds count, and we have the opportunity to pause and use a few of them to respond in a way that serves the bigger picture.

BOOT ON THE OTHER FOOT

Six years and countless flying hours later, I had been promoted in the RAF and was a flight commander on a squadron. The role of the flight commander is akin to middle management in a civilian company. I reported to the squadron commander and, together with two other flight commanders, was accountable for the day-to-day running of the squadron.

I had been given the task of leading a detachment of around 40 aircrew members and maintenance engineers. Equipped with three air-refuelling aircraft, we had relocated to an airbase in Scotland to participate in a week-long military exercise. This was my first time leading such a deployment, and I was keen to ensure it all went to plan.

Unfortunately, the news I received on the first morning following our arrival in Scotland suggested this was not going to be the case: my two most senior maintenance engineers had failed to report for duty. They were the supervisors for my team of technicians – without them, the planes would not be going anywhere. This was not a good start.

It turned out the two men in question – let's call them Dan and Matt – had overslept after enjoying a night out in the local town. I sent someone out to look for them, and they finally showed up almost two hours late. This was unacceptable. I was far from pleased. The question was how I should deal with the situation. I kept them both waiting in a room adjacent to my office while I thought about it.

I reasoned Dan and Matt would know they had screwed up and would likely be expecting me to shout and tear into them. In truth, I was anxious. I had never had to deal with this type of situation before. These two guys, although junior to me in rank, were senior in the number of years they'd served in the military. They were also much older than me, which I felt didn't help. And I was conscious I would need to rely on them for the rest of the week – we had to work together to complete our mission.

I had to find some way to appropriately admonish them for their behaviour and for the poor example they had set the men and women on their team, who looked up to them for leadership. But I needed to do it in a way that had them retain a sense of belonging. If I didn't manage this, afterwards they would feel resentment towards me and an unwillingness to fully engage in our task. That sentiment has no place on an effective team, and certainly not where flying and safety are involved.

One of the benefits of the military system is that those in senior ranks are reassigned every two to three years. This means everyone gets exposed to different leadership styles – both the good and the not so good – which gives them the opportunity to explore and find their own style, based on their experiences of others.

Although this was early in my journey of leadership, I knew shouting and yelling at people in these situations was not me. I also remembered some advice I'd been given a few years previously: when reprimanding someone, ensure they leave the room focused on *what you've said* rather than *how you've said it*. In other words, if all they remember is you screaming and shouting at them, it's missed the point. Having cleared my thoughts, I called for Dan and Matt to be marched into my office.

What sticks in my mind to this day is how much they were shaking as they stood to attention in front of me. I really hadn't expected that at all. While it didn't change how I would approach the conversation, it confirmed to me that they were taking their situation seriously. If they had stood there with smirks on their faces, it would have been a very different story.

Meanwhile, they had no way of knowing how much I, seated as I was behind a solid desk, was also shaking. They were probably preoccupied with the thought of how I had the power to take action that would seriously set back their careers.

What I said to them didn't take long. I quietly and calmly asked them each to explain why they had been late that morning. I listened as Dan and Matt confirmed what I already knew, taking full responsibility for their actions and apologizing for their unacceptable lapse of judgement. As their voices trailed off, I allowed silence to fall as I weighed up the two human beings trembling in front of me. It was time for me to use my judgement.

In a measured voice, I reminded them that they, as the senior maintenance engineers and supervisors, set the tone for the team they led. Their behaviour was completely unacceptable for people of their rank and position. They had let me down, their team down, and themselves down. I expected better.

I asked them if they had anything else to say. They reiterated their apology and committed to make up for their behaviour in the days that followed. I told them I looked forward to it, dismissed them, and they marched out of my office.

THE OPPORTUNITY

I didn't realize it at the time, but the way I dealt with Dan and Matt's behaviour created an opportunity. It would have been fully justified for me to have taken more formal action that would have negatively affected their careers. Instead, I created the space for them to take a step up and choose to lead.

During the rest of the week, I couldn't have asked for more from them. They went above and beyond to ensure the aircraft were serviceable and ready to fly. They solved maintenance problems effectively and led their team of engineers admirably. Our deployment to Scotland was a great success. For the remainder of my time as a flight commander, whenever I needed to deploy with aircraft away from our home base, Dan or Matt would be my first choice as engineering supervisor. They never let me down again. It was clear they felt a degree of loyalty and gratitude towards me, perhaps in a way similar to what I felt towards Jimmy Jewell after screwing up several years before. More importantly, they felt loyalty to their team and what was expected of them as leaders.

IT TAKES PRACTICE

Despite years of facing tough conversations, I still don't find it easy, and it takes a lot of thought and planning. Having to talk with someone when they've made a mistake is difficult to do well, especially since different people respond in different ways.

A close friend of mine, Mike, is the bursar at one of the Oxford University colleges. He runs the team that makes the college function, from student accommodation to catering, security, and building maintenance, and everything in between. I've known Mike for many years, having served with him in the RAF. He's an excellent Jumpseat Leader who is totally committed to lifting others up and helping them grow. Perhaps it's little wonder he thrives in working for an organization designed around doing exactly that.

Among his many skills, Mike is someone I respect for his ability to have tough conversations in service of lifting others up. He seems to me to be a master in this, with a natural ability to find the right words and appropriate tone. It's such an important skill for any leader, and I wanted to learn Mike's secret so I could improve. We met for lunch, and I asked him about how he was able to tackle these conversations with such ease.

Showing natural humble confidence, Mike seemed genuinely surprised when I said I saw him as an expert in this. He explained that, ahead of a tough conversation, he would often lie awake at night, rehearsing all the possible ways he could approach the situation and the likely outcomes. To Mike, having tough conversations is, well, tough. What's key to his ability to do this so effectively is his belief in the potential of others. His motivation to take on any tough conversations is because he wants the other person to be the best version of themselves.

SPIRAL UP

Mike's explanation gets to the nub of how we can best deal with mistakes as a Jumpseat Leader. It calls on us to care enough to invest our time. It's relatively easy to rip into someone when they have made an error. But this reaction usually comes from our own fear. We fear how someone's mistakes may affect our life, livelihood, status, or reputation. When fear is driving us, it can cause us to spiral downward. Our negative reaction will no doubt also cause the person to feel cast out and deflated, and to have their sense of belonging undermined. This in turn can diminish their engagement and the contribution they are willing to make going forward. A downward spiral can have ramifications way into the future.

In the critical seconds before we start a tough conversation, we can choose for what follows to become an opportunity for positive growth. Does this mean that we always go easy on people when they make a mistake? Not at all. We must be guided by how much *they care* about what they have done and the impact it has had. And if they don't care enough, perhaps that says more about our leadership and the environment we create than it does about them.

—— CONSIDER THIS ——

When anyone on a team makes a mistake, it's an opportunity to create a spiral up and avoid a spiral down. We need to be ready to pause and resist any natural tendency to react, often driven by the fear of our life, livelihood, status, or reputation being threatened.

◆ LEARNING TO FLY

Consider this: How we treat ourselves is usually how we treat others.

How do you view your own mistakes? Do you immediately try to fix them? Do you hide them? Do you pause before criticizing yourself? Take note of your actions and feelings.

Mistakes are unavoidable. We are human. Show yourself some grace, take a deep breath, and then take action.

The next time someone lets you down, take a moment to consider how you want your conversation with them to end. Do you want them to remember *what you said* so they have the opportunity to learn and make it right? Or do you want them to remember the *way you said it*, which will likely make only you feel better?

◆ FLYING

Consider this: As you take on more responsibilities and work with more people, there is more room for error.

The next time you need to have a tough conversation, take some time to consider what you are going to say and how the other person may respond. Play out different scenarios in your head, taking into account the long-term outcome you're seeking, not just the immediate result.

Be guided by what you stand for. This will allow you to be better prepared for the conversation and to act from a place of continuing to nurture a sense of belonging.

◆ TEACHING OTHERS TO FLY

Consider this: The next time a public mistake is made, use it as an opportunity to lift that person up in front of everyone.

Show your team that mistakes can happen, and when the choice is made to correct it together, everyone prospers and continues to feel they belong.

◆ LEADING FROM THE JUMPSEAT

Consider this: The next time you sense someone is on a downward spiral, help them to see it can be an opportunity for positive growth.

Sit down and listen to them. Relate to them and, if possible, highlight a time in your life that mirrors what's going on in theirs.

Explain the steps needed and the time it took, so they can begin to see the possibility of their own upward path.

Chapter 12

Handing Over Control

Welcome to your new job. Before we start, I'd like to talk to you about how the company works and the inspiration behind what we do. We are a purpose-driven organization and we are mission-led. Our purpose is to work towards a world where everyone has total freedom to be who they want to be, without judgement. Our mission is to be the world's number-one destination for fashion-loving twenty-somethings. You might ask me to define that, but I'm not going to since it's a restless mission that we should never, ever finish. It's like following the North Star: we'll never get there but we'll keep following it. So, I won't define it but I'll give you some segues along the way.

Our target is to expand our business to be many multiples bigger than it is today. But what I want you to understand is our values that guide our journey. The first of those is I want you to be *authentic*: you've been chosen for your talent, passion, and enthusiasm. All I ask is that you bring the best version of that to work every day. Next, I want you to be *brave*. Bravery in everything you do and to have bravery from the start. Don't forget to turn left when everyone else turns right, because by turning left you might find something interesting. I also want you to be *creative* in everything you do. We are only selling clothes. Let's do everything we do in a creative way and have fun with it. Lastly, I want you to have *discipline*. This isn't about death by key performance indicators or spreadsheets. It's about honing your craft. Like the rock band who gets its first album based on absolute passion and talent, but then gets ten platinum discs by honing their craft. Every sports star, every creative – everyone hones their craft through discipline.

So, we're purpose-driven, mission-led, and guided by those four values. There's one more aspect that's really important to understand why we do what we do and how we do it. That is our approach to fashion is with integrity: about people, products, packaging, and the planet. It's embedded in what we do. Everything I've just described talks about behaviours – behaviours that create an inclusive culture. These are not optional: they bind us together and are a part of who we are.

THE NARRATIVE ABOVE is taken word for word from a catch-up call I had in March 2021 with Nick Beighton, CEO of ASOS, the global fashion and cosmetics retailer. Completely unrehearsed and with no advance warning of the question, this was Nick's response when I asked him what he would say to me if I were a new employee on my first day.

ASOS was founded in 2000. Nick joined the company in 2009 as CFO and became CEO a little over five years later. Based entirely online, ASOS has, at the time of writing, grown to become a multi-billion-dollar business, serving customers in over 200 countries and territories. They hold 85,000 distinct types of item for sale. That equates to over 400,000 products. Every week they bring 5,000 new products live onto their website, ready for sale – around 80 every working hour. Each of these has to be photographed in their studios and have descriptions written, edited, and published. Of course, the company also has to coordinate the stock and ensure the logistics are in place to deliver across the world. Before any of this happens, teams within ASOS need to find and curate the products they want to sell. They offer over 850 different brands, together with their own, in clothing, footwear, and accessories. To bring all this to market, it takes an army of around 4,000 full-time employees, whose average age is just twenty-seven.

Twenty-seven. When I heard this, it seemed to go against everything many have to say about our incoming workforce. Nick had my undivided attention. I wanted to know, *How is all this possible?*

ASOS believes in a world where you have the freedom to be you, without judgement. They want to encourage their customers to be brave and grab life as the extraordinary adventure it is. ASOS sees their role as helping to make sure everyone has an equal chance to discover all the amazing things *they're* capable of, regardless of their background, race, culture, or gender. Through the very powerful medium of fashion, ASOS gives its customers the opportunity to explore and uncover who they are and how they fit into the world, and to have the confidence to express that. In other words, to find how they belong. That goes for its employees too.

To draw all these moving parts together against super-tight deadlines demands discipline and precision. To an outsider taking a stroll, as I did, through the corridors of their London headquarters, it looks at first almost chaotic. There were clothes samples, shoes, and fabrics covering desks; floor-to-ceiling shelves stuffed with products; and rails upon rails of hangers. Occasionally, I'd find small groups of people huddled together on the floor, chatting animatedly around sketches of new designs. In another part of the building there were six fully equipped studios, with models working in tag teams to keep photographers clicking. Alongside this, others tapped away at high-end graphic workstations to ensure the products shot in the morning appeared on the website that afternoon.

As Nick explained to me, the faster they can get products through the studio, the more efficient the process becomes, and the more times they can serve their customers.

ASOS holds the growth of their people as a key enabler for their business. They invest in creating a sense of belonging, in which everyone can have the confidence to show up as themselves while also staying true to the ASOS mission. This creates the environment in which people want to step up and take responsibility for their work and the processes involved.

Guided by Nick, ASOS opens the door to handing over as much control as possible, including to the most junior employee. While the tempo is exceptionally high, everyone I met seemed energized and focused because there's a sense they are the ones flying the plane. It is their hands on the controls.

OH, THIS IS NORMAL

During my visit to their headquarters, Nick took me for lunch in the company restaurant. A bright and welcoming open-plan space, the facility operated with the same pace and efficiency as the rest of the building.

We joined the queue and stood in line with everyone else. The atmosphere was buzzing, with colleagues chatting animatedly to one another about their work. While they smiled and acknowledged Nick, there was no break in their conversation. They clearly felt relaxed and able to continue being themselves. This was so different, I thought, from many companies I've visited, where everyone stops talking when the management enters the room, or steps back in deference as those most senior in rank briskly make their way towards their reserved dining area.

As we waited in line, there seemed to be a spike of energy to one side of the restaurant, just ahead of where we were standing. A small group had started to jump up and down excitedly, waving balloons and banners. I asked Nick what was going on.

"Oh, this is normal," he said. "It looks like a new product launch. It happens quite often over lunchtime. It helps spread the message among our own people and informally celebrates what the individual teams have accomplished."

As we moved closer, I could see a lot of work had gone into the mini event, with what was clearly a big deal with a well-known brand. Those on the project team were showing their colleagues the new products, with some of them striking poses as they pretended to model the new line on themselves.

What struck me was how relaxed Nick was. I got the impression he'd had no direct involvement with the launch. He knew his people were all aligned to their purpose and mission. He trusted them to figure out what they needed to do and deliver. This mirrored what I'd seen around the whole building – it was like watching a bunch of planes take off, each with their own captain, with Nick there simply to make sure they had what they needed to get off the ground.

RESPONSIBILITY VERSUS ACCOUNTABILITY

There's little worse than being told you have control and then having it almost immediately taken away from you.

I remember this happening to me when I was trying to find my feet as a new aircraft captain. I was flying a military plane with an experienced senior examiner – let's call him Mark – who was acting as my copilot, exactly as I would do for Calum many years later. We had just taken off from the island of Ascension, a tiny speck of land that lies in the middle of the Atlantic Ocean, between Africa and South America.

We'd barely left the ground when, to my surprise, Mark said, "I have control" and took over flying the aircraft.

What I didn't know at the time was that he had agreed with the air traffic controllers to do a flypast of the tower before we set course for the UK – something I would have expected him to brief me about beforehand. He obviously wanted a bit of fun himself, but the way he went about it had a negative impact on me. The rest of the crew knew about the plan, but I didn't. I felt left out of the loop and undermined in my role as aircraft captain. I felt I didn't belong. While I'm sure that wasn't Mark's intent, it's exactly what can happen when we use our authority and inadvertently sabotage the responsibility others have taken on.

When a person chooses to take responsibility for their work and actions, we call that ownership. For someone to know they own something, it requires us to hand over control to them. That is not always easy.

When someone is clear about the picture on the box and has the necessary skills, we need to get out of the way and let them take their place at the helm. As they do so, they feel an increase in the contribution they're making, and their sense of belonging builds.

When people choose to take responsibility, they start to lead themselves without the need for a manager or supervisor to chivvy them along. This is when we can create *velocity* in a team – that is, speed with direction. This is the exact outcome I saw happening at ASOS, and exactly what was taken away from me by Mark.

Responsibility is the more powerful twin of accountability. While the two terms are often used interchangeably, from a leadership perspective it can help if we distinguish between them.

Accountability is what we might see in an employment contract. It's what we expect an individual to deliver, and people will be *held to account* if they don't. We *give* accountability to individuals on our team.

Responsibility is different – it's like looking through the other end of the telescope. Responsibility can only be *taken*, and it's a personal choice whether or not to do so.

While we might impose accountability on someone, we can't force them to take responsibility. We can only create the opportunity and then give them the space to step into it. For example, we can make a teenager accountable for putting their laundry in the basket, but it's only when they choose to take responsibility for doing so that it gets done without our constant intervention. Similarly, in business we might make a manager accountable for a project, governed by stringent performance indicators and constraints. However, it's only when that individual chooses to take responsibility for fully delivering the project that it will likely happen, and those performance indicators will be seen as an opportunity rather than a burden. If they don't feel responsible for the outcome, their lack of commitment will almost certainly deliver poorer results. They will then likely blame others for any failings or might just decide to quit altogether.

A STATE OF MIND

Being responsible is a **state of mind** – an attitude. When choosing to be responsible extends across a group, it becomes part of the culture.

When our young kids play out in the street with their friends, as parents we are accountable for their safety. And yet if we see danger, such as cars or maybe a stranger paying too much interest, we take responsibility to protect the whole group of children, not just our own.

On a large construction site, there will be someone formally accountable for safety, but the site will only be free from incidents when everyone chooses to take responsibility for the safety and well-being of each other and of themselves. There will then be a universal willingness to step up and intervene if someone is about to risk injury through their actions, such as taking a potentially dangerous shortcut to complete a task.

A team run on accountability alone is not as effective, agile, motivated, or creative as one that includes those who take personal responsibility. Most of us instinctively know this. For people to choose responsibility, what's often missing is a sufficient sense of belonging. We know we're in an accountability culture when, if something goes wrong, people immediately seek to blame others.

When something goes wrong in a culture of responsibility, people come together to figure out how they can help to resolve the issue and how they may work better together in the future.

DELEGATION, NOT ABDICATION

A Jumpseat Leader needs to nurture an environment in which people are willing to take responsibility, since without it, effective delegation cannot happen.

We are unlikely to delegate unless we feel we can rely on that person to take responsibility for completing what we have asked of them. When we delegate, it frees up our time and energy to focus on those things only we can do, and then have the opportunity to do. Importantly, effective delegation strengthens the sense of belonging, by giving people more opportunity to contribute. Belonging – responsibility – delegation – belonging: a generative cycle is created when we choose to hand over control.

When I took over command of my RAF squadron, I remember being advised, with typical military humour, to *Delete, delegate, or die!* In other words, identify and get rid of those things that aren't important (the equivalent of spam that lands in our inbox), and delegate as much as you can of the rest. The alternative would be to sink under the weight of it all. However, delegation can be scary, particularly when it involves something that is critical or otherwise important to us. Fear can creep in, and we can end up either micro-managing or, at the other extreme, abdicating responsibility. To abdicate is to step away and completely disown the process and outcome, blaming others if it all goes wrong. Equally, we can't use delegation to avoid taking responsibility for tasks we don't like. That's a surefire way to erode engagement and mutual respect, and weaken any sense of belonging. Effective delegation takes practice.

In Chapter 7 I shared the story of flying into Nairobi, when the wheels failed to lower and we were faced with crash-landing the aircraft. The captain, Tony, delegated the task of executing the crash-landing to me, his copilot. I was appropriately trained and capable, and throughout the emergency, Tony continued to show up in support of me. He let me get on with it, without micromanaging. And yet he didn't *abdicate* his responsibility for the plane and everyone on board. With me taking care of the flying, it freed Tony up to think about events beyond the crash-landing, such as the likely evacuation of passengers and coordination with the local emergency services.

Effective delegation enhances our own capacity to think and plan. Nick Beighton shared with me that he sees delegation as a force multiplier and that we should practise delegating to the lowest level we can. It ensures that we, as leaders, don't become the bottleneck – the drag on the system. When delegating, Nick will explain first what his role in the project will be, why the project is important, and how it fits into the overall purpose and mission of the company. He will then ask the other person to go away and reflect before coming back to him with a request for the resources they need. At this point they will also discuss and agree how often Nick will check in on the project and how fast it will move forward. He then lets them get on with it.

Nick's view of delegation mirrors the approach I've experienced in the military. As a squadron commander, I would first ensure that those I was asking to complete the task were appropriately trained and equipped. I would explain what I needed the individual or team to do and the outcome they needed to achieve. Vitally, I would talk about *why* the task was important, the timelines involved, and how the task fitted into the overall plan or mission. It was essential for everyone involved to have an appreciation of the bigger picture, since it would allow them to flex and adjust how they went about the task if circumstances changed, and still achieve the outcome. Without this broader perspective, their actions might have adversely affected others outside of their team. I would then take a step back and allow them to figure out how to deliver, while remaining available to offer advice or support if needed.

Increasingly, what I discovered was that people would come forward with their own ideas for projects or actions they wanted to pursue. They stepped up without being asked. All I needed to do was to ensure they remained aware of the wider context and had what they needed to deliver.

Delegation is a two-way street. We might delegate a task to one of our team, but to be effective, that person needs to choose to take responsibility. And that only occurs when they feel a strong sense of belonging.

IN TIMES OF CRISIS

There are rare occasions when, as leaders, we need to be very direct and leave no room for doubt, confusion, or misinterpretation over what we need from our team. There is only one context in which this is warranted: in an emergency or crisis, and only when we already know what actions need to be taken. I'll call this approach **command and control**.

The engine fire that occurred on United Airlines Flight 328 shortly after it took off from Denver, Colorado, on 20th February 2021 is an example of a very rare event and one that pilots train extensively to deal with. It's not a time for the captain to start asking the crew how they feel they should handle the situation. Instead, the captain will give a very clear command such as, "Fire drill, number two engine". The crew then responds in the way they have been trained to do, with a series of predetermined actions. The United Airlines flight landed safely and no one was hurt – a demonstration of how the process really works.

Most of us are familiar with similar actions when our feet are firmly on the ground, such as building fire drills.

Several years ago, I was running a workshop for the leadership team of Cuestamoras, a company in Costa Rica. It was shortly before we were due to break for lunch, with the buffet laid out and ready to go. Suddenly, with no warning, an earthquake struck and the building began to shake violently. The alarm sounded, and within moments, the floor marshals appeared, using predetermined *immediate actions* to direct everyone to the safe muster area. The response was very proficient and well practised. There was no discussion. No debate.

When time is critical, where any delay would risk the situation becoming worse, the command-and-control approach works well to initiate a team's response to a crisis. An office evacuation, a major commercial oil spill, a corporate data breach, or an intranet hack – all of these demand a rapid response. Each of them can be anticipated, planned, and trained for. This ensures the team responds appropriately, rather than reacting inappropriately, driven by fear and panic. We control the fear by using our authority to tell – or command – our people what to do.

After these immediate actions have been carried out, those in authority need to move quickly back towards delegation and building an environment in which others feel able to contribute to solving the problem, just as Gene Kranz did when navigating the Apollo 13 crisis.

If the command-and-control approach is maintained beyond those immediate actions, it will limit innovation, create a "wait to be told" culture, and ultimately lead to disengagement. It's also really exhausting as a leader, not to mention practically impossible, to try to track and direct every last action. It can work well in a crisis, but over the long term, a command-and-control approach of telling people what to do undermines leadership.

FOUR RED LIGHTS

The more we are able to delegate, the more we lift others up and the more equipped they become to lead. The challenge for a Jumpseat Leader is to know when to step in again when things start to go awry. How do we know when that time has come? How do we intervene in a way that doesn't burst the balloon of confidence of the other person, which could take weeks or months to build back up?

When we feel something is really important, human nature will naturally drive us to step in and intervene sooner rather than later whenever we see a problem or threat. But if we want to harness the full collective genius of our team and give them the opportunity to lead, we need to build the muscle that enables us to let go of that urge to control.

We should certainly train our people in the skills they need. And yet the journey of our own lives has taught us that we learn through experience, which inevitably means making some mistakes along the way. We all likely have memories of when others had faith in our ability and gave us the opportunity to step up, and of how exhilarating, fulfilling, and energizing that felt. They've also been there to help pick us up and move forward when we've taken a fall.

While professional pilots train extensively in simulators to learn how to land aircraft in all kinds of poor weather, there is no substitute for the adrenaline and focus that occur when doing it for real. When you're in the air, it's not possible to hit *pause and reset* if you get it wrong. As captain, it can be very tempting to take over the controls from a junior pilot, for example when the weather conditions are really challenging, or when the pilot is not flying as well as you could. But if you do step in, that pilot will never build the experience they need to be a captain in the future when there is no longer anyone else to take over the controls.

I found myself faced with that judgement with a junior pilot – let's call him John – who was flying our large passenger jet as we started our approach into Gander International Airport. The weather was quite poor, with blustery winds making the approach more challenging than usual. This is quite common for Gander, perched as it is on the large island of Newfoundland, off the east coast of mainland Canada.

John began well, then, a few miles out from the runway, we started to see what are known as the precision approach path indicators, or PAPIs. These are a set of four lights to the side of the runway, which can independently shine red or white, to help pilots recognize if they are approaching at the correct angle to land safely. The aim is to be able to see two red lights and two white. If the pilot sees three white lights and one red, they're too high. Three red lights and only one white, they're too low. Four reds, and they are way too low and could risk hitting the ground or an obstacle before the runway.

Initially, I could see two red lights and two white – all good. But then John allowed the aircraft to descend more quickly than it should, and the PAPIs changed to three red and one white – not so good. I called out to John that he was low and needed to take action. John acknowledged but didn't take the action needed, which would have been to increase power from the engines.

While concerned, I wanted John to have the opportunity to correct his error before I intervened. A few seconds later, the PAPIs changed to four red lights. Although still several hundred feet above the ground, we were now getting dangerously low to make a safe landing. I alerted John to apply more power. He didn't. Even then, I didn't take over the controls. Instead, I nudged the engine throttles forward a little, calling it out as I did so. We quickly regained the correct approach angle, and John completed a smooth landing.

There were several points on this approach where I could have taken over the flying and chose not to. I knew that John had to learn. By taking over early, I would have popped John's balloon of confidence. It was only when I judged we were about to reach the point beyond which I couldn't recover the situation safely that I stepped in. I needed to make the shift from my role as a great follower, supporting John, to my broader role of captain, with the added responsibility of ensuring the safety of everyone on board.

John learned from the experience and the debrief afterwards. Later in his career, he went on to become a successful captain and instructor pilot, helping junior pilots to develop their skills, in just the same way as I had helped him to develop his.

We can all probably think of times when we've stepped in early and taken over from someone on our team, justifying it as the easiest, quickest, or least risky thing to do. Like when we write the email to an important client ourselves rather than having the account manager write a draft and working with them to refine it. We might also recall moments when we've had control taken from us, and how frustrated and undermined we've felt. Like when we were learning to drive, and the instructor took over when the traffic got busy. And we may be fortunate and have memories of when others had faith in our ability and gave us the opportunity to grow, and of how good that felt. Like the first time we closed a big deal on our own.

When the actions of others, despite their best intentions, have the potential to affect our life, livelihood, status, or reputation, it takes courage to wait before we intervene. It takes courage to wait until we see our equivalent of four red lights. When we do find that courage, that's when true growth in our team occurs and we plant the seed for others to step up and become leaders too.

Judging when to take back control can be difficult, so here are some helpful suggestions to reflect on before stepping in and taking back control:

◆ **Recognize that the urge to step in is going to happen**

It's human nature to want to control those things that are really important to us. When we acknowledge this, we can prepare for it.

◆ **Question whether the urge is driven by love or fear**

When we recognize the urge to step in, we should ask ourselves if it comes from our ego or vanity rising up, or whether by stepping in we will genuinely be in service of others.

◆ **Consider whether it is time to choose the many over the one**

Do the needs of our team, company, or cause warrant bursting the balloon of the person we're about to take over from? Once that balloon is popped, it can take a long time to recover, if it can recover at all.

◆ **Know your decision point**

When will you get to your four red lights? How far can you allow the situation to continue before it goes beyond your ability to salvage it?

◆ **Choose the smallest intervention**

When we reach our four-red-lights decision point, it doesn't necessarily mean we need to completely take over. Perhaps a small prompt or nudge is all that's required.

◆ **Decide whether the outcome really matters**

Sometimes, when we take a moment to pause and reflect on the bigger picture, it gives us the chance to re-evaluate how important a moment is. Will it matter in a day, a week, or six months from now? Is it worth the trade-off, given the potential positive effect on the individual if we choose not to intervene?

HOLD THE SPACE

Each year around 20 percent of the ASOS workforce chooses to leave. Interestingly, a good percentage of those later return to work at ASOS, bringing their new-found knowledge, experience, and energy back to the organization. Nick encourages this, since during their time away many go on to explore the world, life's adventures, or other companies in the industry.

"It's OK," he reflects. "Our people know they always have a place back here."

Nick makes it very clear to his people, from their first day working at ASOS, how they can belong. Equally, he ensures he is constantly reminded too. How does he do that? He keeps the big picture in front of him, or – in this case – in his back pocket. As I was leaving, Nick pulled out what I thought was a business card and handed it to me. Rather than his contact details, it had some text overlaid on his own photo. It read:

After ballerina Michaela DePrince's talk at the Zeitgeist conference, I complimented her on her dress. She replied, "It's from ASOS. It gives me confidence – I feel I can do anything when wearing it." This made me incredibly proud and humble to work at ASOS. – Nick Beighton, CEO

Was Nick directly a part of every step of the process to get the dress into this woman's hands? No. But by working together, he knows his team made it happen, and this was only made possible by handing over control to them so they could create many more moments like this for others.

All we can do is create opportunity, hold the space for our people to step up, and be there to support them as they take over the controls. The more we get out of the way, the more they can see there is an empty seat they can fill. And that's the essence of Jumpseat Leadership.

—— CONSIDER THIS ——

Handing over control is an inherent part of being a Jumpseat Leader, and it calls on us to learn to delegate effectively. Effective delegation can only be sustained if those on our team choose to take responsibility. And they will only choose to take responsibility if they feel a sense of belonging.

◆ LEARNING TO FLY

Consider this: Notice how it's easier to take responsibility for something when you know and care about it – when you feel you belong. Notice too how choosing to take responsibility creates more opportunity.

Start by choosing to take responsibility for your own life, career, and growth.

The next time you're asked to be accountable for an outcome, think about how you can demonstrate that you are going to go a step further by taking responsibility and ownership over the task.

◆ FLYING

Consider this: Practise effective delegation informally, even if you do not formally lead a team.

Notice when others are particularly energized about a shared task, as this might be an opportunity to delegate. Guard against abdication. When you are given accountability for a task, choose to take responsibility.

Seek to clarify and understand the outcome within the context of the bigger picture. Raise your hand if you feel you need help.

The next time you're feeling overwhelmed with what you have on your plate, try delegating. Be certain to delegate to those who have the skills, understand the ins and outs, and know why the task is valuable.

◆ TEACHING OTHERS TO FLY

Consider this: Deepen your knowledge of the skills, ability, and attributes of your team – this knowledge will help you to delegate better.

When delegating, be clear on what you're asking, the desired outcome and why it matters, and that the person you are delegating to has the necessary skills and training. Guard against abdication.

The next time you're in front of your team, take the opportunity to discuss the context. Ask each of them if they understand their role and how it fits into the overall whole. If there's any confusion, take the time to ensure everyone is clear on how they belong.

◆ LEADING FROM THE JUMPSEAT

Consider this: Support others in the art of delegation.

Guard against backseat driving, where we hand over control but continue to interfere and undermine the other person's decisions and actions. If this happens frequently, there is insufficient trust, insufficient training, or both.

The next time you have the urge to take over the controls, think first about your four-red-lights point. If you do end up needing to intervene, try to see how little you can do to right the situation. This will allow those you are working with to maintain their confidence and continue to learn.

Now Consider This

FOR FOUR LONG months, Flight Sergeant Ewing had bellowed orders at the Royal Air Force officer recruits. Those recruits included me, then a thin and wiry 20-year-old.

As the drill sergeant for the military college, Ewing's job was to teach the future junior officers standing before him what was expected of them, while instilling a strong sense of self-discipline. He wanted us to be the best leaders we could be, even though he was fully aware that, when we graduated, we would outrank him and he would be required to follow *our* orders.

It is common for British, American, and many other major military organizations to expect young officers, immediately after graduating from military college, to lead teams of people who are senior to them in both age and experience. But during initial training, recruits are at the mercy of those known as non-commissioned officers, such as Flight Sergeant Ewing.

This was the very situation we faced during those months in 1983 at RAF College Cranwell. Ewing called the shots, and my fellow recruits and I would jump at every order he barked, willing to endure any hardship, our sights set firmly on the prize of becoming officers. On the blustery afternoon of 19th October that year, though, everything would change. Our training was complete, and it was graduation day.

Following a formal military drill parade, the final part of the graduation ceremony saw each of us being awarded a commissioning scroll. This is a formal document, signed by Her Majesty The Queen, signifying that the named person is now a commissioned officer.

As the ceremonial music played, we slow-marched in single file up the steps of the imposing main entrance of College Hall.

As we were handed our scrolls, there, at the top of the steps, was Flight Sergeant Ewing. For months, he had been the person we all looked towards to lead us. During that time, he had lifted us up to become leaders ourselves. Now he stood smartly to attention, his hand raised in a crisp salute, acknowledging each of us as we filed past, with a clear "Sir!" or "Ma'am!", in recognition of the authority we now held.

With his job done, he willingly took a step back, ready to follow with pride the young leaders he had shaped. Soon after this day, his mind would turn towards his next batch of officer recruits.

GIVE IT A GO

You may not have a Flight Sergeant Ewing lifting you up or a commissioning scroll signed by your head of state. But in reality, you need neither of these things to choose to become a Jumpseat Leader. All you need to do is make the commitment to begin.

In some aspects of your life, you might already be **Teaching others to fly** or **Leading from the Jumpseat**, perhaps in your role as a business leader or senior manager. If so, consider using the examples, language, and ideas in this book to become more intentional and to further enhance how you build other Jumpseat Leaders within your team.

In other areas, you may be at the beginning of your journey, possibly having just taken on new responsibilities; changed careers; or developed a new complex skill such as sailing, scuba diving, or mountaineering. In these cases, the ideas in this book will have a different relevance, as you will be **Learning to fly** before getting into your stride and **Flying**.

Wherever you are in your journey, pick one of the **Consider this** ideas and give it a go. The idea could apply in the context of work, being a parent, or simply having the courage to lead yourself. Reflect on what is really important to you; what are your non-negotiables, your stands? How might you use those stands to accomplish something beyond what you already do, to stand at the top of the mountain and commit to the outcome, even when you don't yet fully know how to get there?

Consider how making a **commitment** will create a warehouse of possibility that invites those around you – your formal team, or others inspired by the commitment you've made – to help you figure out the answers.

Consider how embracing **humble confidence** will create the environment in which you can draw on the collective genius your people have to offer.

Consider how you will create a sense of **belonging** for those around you, so they too might choose to take responsibility for the outcome and contribute more.

THE OPPORTUNITY

Being able to share past experiences, as I have in this book, might give the impression that I was always intentionally practising Leading from the Jumpseat.

The truth, of course, is that at the time I had little idea I was doing this. When my son wanted his powerful Suzuki motorcycle, I didn't realize I was using my stands to help figure out how to move forward. When I briefed my people in the desert just before the start of the Iraq War in 2003, I didn't realize the power of painting a simple, clear picture. When sitting behind Calum on the flight out of San Francisco, or leading my team of specialists on a £13 billion project, I didn't realize I was practising Jumpseat Leadership.

Many years after leaving the RAF, it was a great privilege to hear from Simon, Al, and Phil how I had helped them rise to become the leaders they are now. There are likely many more occasions since when I have used Jumpseat Leadership without realizing it. Often, we won't know the full extent of the difference we have made. Looking back, while I may not have seen myself at the time as a Jumpseat Leader, I know I was always committed to lifting others up. And when we make that commitment, the possibilities it creates are limitless.

Leading from the Jumpseat is a lifelong practice. It's challenging, and it takes courage. I've learned that, as Jumpseat Leaders, what we cause to happen has the power to live on long beyond the moment. We won't always get it right – and that's okay. It's our intention and the overall trend over time that count, together with a willingness to acknowledge that when we trip, it's worth getting up, reflecting on what we've learned, and trying again.

Here's the opportunity you now have: the ideas and guidance in this book can act as stepping stones to help you to become a better Jumpseat Leader than you already are. While I'm still learning and practising, my hope is that what I've written will accelerate your own development. And I hope that you will lift others up by Leading from the Jumpseat.

The sooner we start, the greater our legacy will be.

LEGACY

On New Year's Day in 2015 I met up with my daughter, Louise, for an orienteering event. Orienteering is a competitive sport, generally held in rugged countryside, in which participants race to find a series of checkpoints, known as controls, marked on a map. The idea is to run and navigate as quickly and accurately as possible. Those with the fastest time win.

Although this sport is designed for individual competitors, Louise and I had decided to run this one together. I'd orienteered for many years, and Louise had completed quite a few events too, although it had been a while for each of us since our last one. We were both a bit rusty and so decided it would be fun to enter as a pair.

We filled out the forms and were given a map to share, along with the list of controls to find. We walked purposefully to the start line, with me (having the most experience) poised to lead off to the first control. But something made me pause and turn to Louise, then hand her the map, the list of controls, and the compass.

"Go on," I said. "You lead. I'll follow you. Show me which way to go."

A little hesitant at first, Louise soon got into her stride. By the third or fourth control, we had started to work effectively as a team, with Louise pointing out which way to go and telling me which terrain features to look for, while I focused on running and spotting the telltale orange and red flags that marked the controls. It was pretty satisfying to see her confidence grow. By the end, we'd developed our technique well together, and we crossed the finish line tired and sweaty, with our relationship further bolstered by conquering the challenge as a team.

I must admit, I felt quite emotional at the end of the event. Looking back on that day, it strikes me how symbolic it was to pass the map and compass to Louise. As her father, I had for years done my best to guide and coach, and to hold the space for her to grow. Sometimes I had got it right; other times less so. And yet she had become a grown woman, hugely capable and confident, able to lead herself and her own life. It was a delight to see. Today she continues to reach higher, to challenge her own limits, and to stand at the top of mountains.

The same is true of her brother – my son, Patrick. While I've long since hung up my pilot flying gloves, I'm delighted that Patrick has chosen to pick up his own. He's currently a pilot in the Royal Navy, and I'm confident he's already much more capable than I was at that stage of my career. Patrick completed some of his early training at the same RAF base where I learned to fly almost 40 years ago. Hearing his stories of once-familiar places reconnects me to those early days. We often find ourselves chatting about the technicalities of flying, or swapping tales of the highs and lows of going through the lengthy flying training process. It was during one such time that Patrick mentioned someone who'd remembered me. I smiled to myself when he told me his name: it was the same four-red-lights John I wrote about in Chapter 12, who had been my copilot flying into Gander International Airport all those years ago. I had lifted him up then, and now he had grown to become an instructor helping to lift up others, including my son.

I feel pride when reflecting on who Louise and Patrick have become as human beings, what drives them, and how they treat others. They have both chosen to reach higher and outside their comfort zones in ways I could not have imagined, developing skills and capabilities beyond my own. It's a joy for me to see them rise – a joy felt by any parent as they see their own children build confidence and grow.

This sense of joy extends beyond immediate family. It's there when I reflect on all those I have seen, over the years, rising to lead themselves and others, many of whom are mentioned in this book. And now I realize that enjoying seeing others succeed is so often a direct result of when we have been at our best as a Jumpseat Leader.

Like Flight Sergeant Ewing, at some point we all take a step back to allow others to lead. When we do, if we have prac-tised Jumpseat Leadership, we will have a legacy that is about other people – how our actions have positively affected their lives, and how we've helped them grow so they can lead. We will have stories of accomplishments driven by love rather than fear, of inspiring others into action, and of support-ing them so they can go on to positively affect the lives of others too.

As Jumpseat Leaders, our legacy is about what happens next when, inevitably, the time comes for us to hand over the controls.

Our legacy is about the delight of seeing other people rise after we have lifted them up. It's about the collection of stories, positive experiences, and upward spirals we leave in our wake.

And possibly the most compelling aspect of Leading from the Jumpseat: as our positive actions inspire others to lead in the same way, we will never really know the full extent of those upward spirals we create – to see how others will become the extraordinary human beings they have the potential to be as they continue to build on our legacy with stories of their own.

Now consider this: what stories will you leave behind?

───── Lifting Others Up ─────

COMMITMENT. HUMBLE CONFIDENCE. BELONGING. It takes all three to write a book, and I've had the opportunity to practise each of them while writing *Leading from the Jumpseat*.

Writing is a challenge, especially if you want anyone to read what you've written. It calls on commitment and a determination to stay connected with the view from the top of the mountain, even when at times you might not be entirely sure how you're going to reach the summit. The editing process is an excellent opportunity to let go of ego and embrace humble confidence. This was particularly the case for me when, after having written 30,000 words, I acted on advice and started all over again.

More than anything, what has made the journey of writing *Leading from the Jumpseat* possible – and enjoyable – has been the people around me. We have all created a shared commitment and worked to nurture a sense of belonging – a sense that we're in this together and giving our all. This part of the book is the opportunity to lift those individuals up for their extraordinary talents and contributions.

Before I shine the spotlight on them, I want to pause for a moment and acknowledge the other people who have influenced my life over the years. Each of them, sometimes without even knowing it, has nudged my thoughts and, more recently, my writing. We are all a result of our experiences, and especially of those moments that involve interaction with other human beings. I've come to realize that even the times that seemed negative or heartbreaking when they occurred have also helped me to evolve how I lead myself and others. All those characters I've mentioned throughout this book have played their part, together with many others who fill my memories.

One chap who likely doesn't know the difference he made to me is Squadron Leader Phil Foster. Phil was the organizer of the event in the first chapter – the one where I stopped several times on the drive to give a talk to the RAF squadron commanders. For two years, Phil had tried to persuade me to give the talk. He couldn't have known at the time how his persistence would enable me to overcome my fears and help create the impetus for this book. This is another example of how we sometimes have no idea of the far-reaching effect our actions can have on others. Phil was the first pebble in the pond, and the ripples continue to spread.

No endeavour starts without a catalyst, and we also all need support and encouragement in order to succeed. While I've been flying around the world, building the experiences and stories you've read about in this book, Claire has been a fantastic mother to our children, Louise and Patrick. Particularly while I was involved in combat operations, with neither of us knowing when or even if I would return, she kept our family together during times of great uncertainty and fear. This must have been one of the most challenging roles for any parent, and yet the remarkable adults Louise and Patrick have become are testament to Claire's leadership skills. Equally impressive, she served as an officer in the RAF and built a subsequent career in a large business. She has been my consistent cheerleader, and the voice of reason that has helped keep me on an even keel. More than that, she has been the solid foundation on which everything has been built over the thirty-plus years of our marriage. She has stayed alongside me even when I've fought depression and lost my way, and I am who I am because of her enduring support. I love her deeply.

We all need a network of friends in life, and I couldn't have wished for better. Simon Marshall, Mike Naworynsky, and David Mead deserve special mention.

I was at school with Simon, and we have always been there for one another through the different stages of life, celebrating the triumphs and lifting each other up when either of us has struggled. He is a champion of people realizing their potential, and he is the master of seeing possibility where others see none.

Mike and I served together in the RAF. He and his wife, Vanessa, have been the most fabulous neighbours and friends, particularly to Claire while I was deployed for the Iraq War; I will be forever grateful. We have all remained close friends ever since. Our children grew up together, and it's a delight to see them carry that friendship on to the next generation.

David Mead and I have worked together, as speakers and facilitators, for the past eleven years. It was David's hunch that ultimately led to my speaking career and the possibilities that have followed since. He's called me out when I've not got it right and lifted me up when I've needed an injection of humble confidence. He's been a constant inspiration as a generous human being, and I couldn't imagine this journey without him.

Then there is my wider circle of friends and colleagues who, while not present every day in my life, have all contributed to who I have become and are a constant reminder of what's possible in this world. Those include A J Egerton, for his sense of duty and honour; Mark McArthur-Christie, for his ability to enrich the experience of life; Janina Bisley, for her connectedness with the world; Paul Mondelli, for staying true to what he believes; Beverley Sweeten-Smith, for her compassion and willingness to embrace the unknown; Rebecca Bailey, for her love of all things; Sharron Mahony, for her courage; Marian Stefani, for her energy, inspiration and service to others.

I'm also fortunate to know many people around the world, whom I consider to be my friends as well as colleagues, past and present: Wajeeha Al Husseini, Sharin Apostolou MacPherson, Rich Diviney, Matt Dunsmoor, Ingrid Eras-Magdalena, Kristen Hadeed, Kim Harrison, Monique Helstrom, Lori Jackson, Anna Lang, Pete Longworth, Ian Scott, Stephen Shedletzky, Simon Sinek, Molly Strong, Jen Waldman, Darren and Melissa Williams. You have all moved and inspired me. I also want to thank the amazing Christina Alessi for her ability to connect and create opportunity. And the entire Chapman & Co team, especially Matt Whiat and Sara Hannah, whose generosity and warmth never cease to amaze me.

And now I turn my thanks to all the people who have made this book happen. Anthony Mattero, literary agent at Creative Artists Agency, whose sage advice and guidance helped steer me along the best path. Kaveh Haerian, whose creativity brought impact to the cover design. Catherine Williams, who designed the internal layout of the text in a way that makes the words on the page flow. My copyeditors, Ilsa Hawtin and Georgina Fradgley, for their meticulous, timely and always diplomatic engagement. Cassandra Smith, who helped shape this book in its early stages. Thanks as well to all those I have not yet mentioned, who read my manuscript and gave such valuable feedback: Alex, Alice, Andy, Jim, Mali, Nick, Ralf, and Susie. A special mention to the wonderful Siobhán Edwards, who read the drafts through the lens of parenthood and shared her insights; and to Joseph, who read the manuscript through the eyes of a current airline pilot and confirmed my flying stories still resonated.

Finally, the greatest thanks to the remarkable team who have been in the trenches with me to bring this book into existence and share it with the world: Jeff Beruan and Ashleigh Riddle.

A quick internet search of Jeff will reveal he is an opera singer of some renown, having performed on stages around the world. It's been a joy to see how he adapted his two decades of on-stage storytelling experience to help me develop the thread of my writing. He used his skill of connecting with an audience to raise my ability to do the same. He was able to take on the roles of **Learning to fly, Flying, Teaching others to fly,** and **Leading from the Jumpseat,** to curate the **Consider this** sections. Above all, Jeff's focus, dedication, and rock-like support have brought a calm to my book-writing adventure. Thank you, my friend.

Ashleigh Riddle is a truly remarkable human being. Over the years, I have seen her grow into a great leader. For this book, she has been the composer of the music and the conductor of the orchestra, while also embracing the dance. She has stood alongside me at the top of the mountain and partnered with me to help figure out all the challenges in front of us. She shows courage and vision beyond her years and sees fear as a catalyst to drive her actions from love. Above all, she has a heart larger than the state of Georgia, USA, where she lives. If you're able to count Ashleigh as a friend, you are indeed fortunate. If you have Ashleigh's support in a challenge, you will prevail.

As I recount all these extraordinary people, and the many others I have met around the world who have contributed to my journey, it fills me with joy. And for me, that joy is the definition of success.